Religion in America

ADVISORY EDITOR

Edwin S. Gaustad

CREED AND DEED

A SERIES OF DISCOURSES

BY

FELIX ADLER, Ph. D.

ARNO PRESS
A NEW YORK TIMES COMPANY
New York • 1972

Reprint Edition 1972 by Arno Press Inc.

Reprinted from a copy in
The Union Theological Seminary Library

RELIGION IN AMERICA - Series II
ISBN for complete set: 0-405-04050-4
See last pages of this volume for titles.

Manufactured in the United States of America

Library of Congress Cataloging in Publication Data

Adler, Felix, 1851-1933.
　Creed and deed.

　　(Religion in America, series II)
　　CONTENTS: Immortality.--Religion.--The new
ideal. [etc.]
　　1. Religion--Addresses, essays, lectures.
2. Ethics--Addresses, essays, lectures. 3. Ethical
culture movement--Addresses, essays, lectures.
I. Title.
BL50.A33　1972　　　　200　　　　76-38430
ISBN 0-405-04051-2

CREED AND DEED

A SERIES OF DISCOURSES

BY

FELIX ADLER, Ph. D.

ἔργῳ κοὐ λόγῳ
—*Aeschylus, Promoth. Vinct. l. 336.*

NEW YORK
PUBLISHED FOR THE SOCIETY FOR ETHICAL CULTURE
BY
G. P. PUTNAM'S SONS
1877

Copyright, 1877
By FELIX ADLER, Ph. D.

PREFATORY NOTICE.

THE lectures contained in the following pages are published by request of the society before which they were delivered. Those on Immortality and Religion have been considerably abridged and condensed. The remainder have been allowed to retain their original form without any serious modification. The First Anniversary Discourse reviews the work of the year, and gives a brief account of the motives which impelled the society to organize and of the general animus by which its labors are directed. The Lecture entitled The Form of the Ideal foreshadows the constructive purpose of the movement. The articles on The Evolution of Hebrew Religion and Reformed Judaism from the *Popular Science Monthly* (*September*, 1876) and the *North American Review* (*July-August* and *September-October*) contain the substance of several of the lectures of last winter's course, and are reprinted in the appendix with the kind consent of the editors. Rigid adherence to the requirements of systematic exposition is neither possible nor desirable in addresses of this kind and has not therefore been attempted.

In giving this volume to the public I gladly embrace the opportunity of expressing my sincere gratitude to those faithful and self-sacrificing friends whose indefatigable labors have gone so far to win for a hazardous venture the promise of assured permanence and satisfactory development.

FELIX ADLER.

New York, September, 1877.

TABLE OF CONTENTS.

		PAGE
I	IMMORTALITY	1
II.	RELIGION	37
III.	THE NEW IDEAL	63
IV.	THE PRIEST OF THE IDEAL	76
V.	THE FORM OF THE NEW IDEAL	90
VI.	THE RELIGIOUS CONSERVATISM OF WOMEN	104
VII.	OUR CONSOLATIONS	118
VIII.	SPINOZA	133
IX.	THE FOUNDER OF CHRISTIANITY	150
X.	THE ANNIVERSARY DISCOURSE	167

APPENDIX.

I.	THE EVOLUTION OF HEBREW RELIGION	183
II.	REFORMED JUDAISM, I II	202
III.	REFORMED JUDAISM, III	218

CREED AND DEED.

I.

IMMORTALITY.

" Not by the Creed but by the Deed."

THE Society which I have the privilege of addressing has been organized with the above for its motto. Some of my hearers have entirely abandoned the tenets of the positive religions; others continue to hold them true, but are discouraged by the lack of spiritual force, the prominence given to mere externals, the barren formalism in the churches and synagogues. We agree in believing that theology is flourishing at the expense of religion. It seems to us that differences in creed are constantly increasing, and will continue to multiply with the growth and differentiation of the human intellect. We perceive that every attempt to settle problems of faith has thus far signally failed, nor can we hope for better results in the future. Certainty even with regard to the essential dogmas appears to us impossible. We do not therefore deny dogma, but prefer to remit it to the sphere of individual conviction with which public associations should have no concern. Far from believing that the doctrines of religion as commonly taught are essential to the well being of society, we apprehend that the disputes concerning the "author of the law" have diverted the attention of men from the law itself, and that the so-called duties toward God too often interfere with the proper performance of our duties toward one another. It were better to insist less upon a right belief, and more upon right action.

In order to find a common basis whereon good men, whether believers or unbelievers, can unite, we look to the moral law itself, whose certainty rests in the universal experience of civilized humanity. We shall hold questions of faith in abeyance, shall endeavor to stimulate the conscience and to this end shall seek to awaken an interest in the grave social problems of our day, which need nothing so much as a vigorous exertion of our moral energies, in order to arrive at a peaceable solution. To broaden and deepen the ethical sentiment in ourselves, and to hold up to the sad realities of the times, the mirror of the ideal life, is the object with which we set out. We do not therefore delude ourselves with the hope that the ideal will ever be fully realized, but are convinced that in aspiring to noble ends the soul will take on something of the grandeur of what it truly admires. Starting with the assumption that the doctrines of religion are incapable of proof, it behooves us to show in one or more instances the fallacy of the arguments upon which they are commonly founded, and we shall begin with the doctrine of IMMORTALITY.

In approaching our subject we are first confronted by the argument from the common consent of mankind. Like the belief in God, the hope of immortality is said to be implanted in every human heart, and the experience of travellers is cited to show that even the most barbarous races have given it expression in some form, however crude. Aside from the fact that the statement, as it stands, is somewhat exaggerated, we will admit that the belief in a future state is widely current among savage tribes. But the value of this testimony becomes extremely doubtful on closer inspection. A brief account of the origin of the conception of soul among our primitive ancestors, will make this plain.

If we observe a child in its sleep, some half articulate word, some cry or gesture occasionally reveals to us the vividness of the dreams with which the little brain is teeming. It is hardly doubtful that the child mistakes the visions of its dream for actual occurrences, and attaches the same reality to these miasmas of the stagnant night as to the clear prospects of daylight reason. Even the adult sometimes finds it difficult to clear his brain of the fancies which occupied it in the hours of sleep. And the test of large experience can alone enable him to distinguish between fact and phantom. I call attention to these facts, because the phenomena of sleep and dreams seem to offer a satisfactory clue to the naïve theories of the lower races concerning death and the after life. The savage indeed is the veritable child-man. His ardent emotions, his crude logic, the eagerness with which he questions the how and wherefore of nature, and the comparative ease with which his simple understanding accepts the most fanciful solutions, all combine to place him on the level of the child.

Aware that the body in sleep is at rest, while at the same time the sleeper is conscious of acting and suffering, visiting distant regions perhaps, conversing with friends, engaging in battle with enemies, the savage reasoned that there must be a man within the man, as it were,—an airy counterfeit of man which leaves its grosser tenement in the night, and in the course of its wanderings experiences whatever the fortunes of the dream may chance to be. Instances are related where the body was prematurely disturbed, the inner man was prevented from returning to his envelope, and death resulted. The shadow cast by the human figure, an attenuated image of man, connected with the body and yet distinct from it, afforded a curious confirmation of this artless theory. The Basutos* affirm that a person having on one occasion incautiously approached the bank of a river, his shadow was seized by a crocodile, and he died in consequence. The story of shadowless or soulless men has been made familiar to modern literature by Chamisso's well known tale.† The spectral man who severs his connection with the body during sleep, remains concealed within it during the hours of waking, and in this manner, the idea of a human soul as distinct from the body, takes its rise.‡ It is easy to see how by extending the analogy, what we call death must have appeared as only another form of sleep, and how the theory of dreams gave rise to a belief in the continuance of life beyond the grave. That sleep and death are twin brothers, was to the primitive man more than mere metaphor. As in sleep, so in death, the body is at rest, but as in sleep, so

---

* The dream theory seems to be the one generally adopted by writers on primitive culture. For an extended account of this subject *vide* the works of Tylor, Lubbock and Bastian, from which the illustrations given in the text are taken.

† Peter Schlemihl.

‡ The soul was believed to be corporeal in nature, only more vague and shadowy than the framework of the body, and distinguished by greater swiftness of locomotion.

also in death, a shade was supposed to go forth capable of acting and suffering, and yearning to return to its former condition. The apparitions of the deceased seen at night by the friends they had left behind, were taken to be real visitations, and corroborated the assumption of the continued existence of the departed. The ghosts of the dead were dreaming phantoms, debarred from permanently returning to their abandoned bodies.

The view we have taken of the origin of the conception of soul is greatly strengthened when we consider the thoroughly material character of the ghost's life after death. The ghost continues to be liable to hunger, pain, cold, as before. But the living have shut it out from their communion; in consequence it hates its former companions, persecutes them where it can, and wreaks its vengeance upon them when they are least prepared to resist it. In a certain district of Germany it was believed that the dead person, when troubled by the pangs of hunger, begins by gnawing its shroud until that is completely devoured, then rising from the grave, it stalks through the village and in the shape of a vampire, sits upon the children in their cradles, and sucks their blood. When sated with the hideous feast, it returns to the churchyard to renew its visits on the succeeding nights. In order to hinder them from using their jaws, it was customary to place

IMMORTALITY.

stones or coins into the mouths of the dead before burial and the most grotesque devices were resorted to, to prevent the much dreaded return of the denizens of the tomb. In the middle ages the corpse was often spiked down to hinder its rising. Among the Hottentots a hole was broken into the wall, through which the corpse was carried from the house, and then carefully covered up, it being the prevailing superstition, that the dead can only reënter by the same way in which they have previously made their exit. Among a certain negro tribe of Africa, the path from the house to the grave was strewn with thorns, in the hope that the ghost would find the path too painful, and desist. As late as 1861, it occurred in a village in Gallicia, that the ghost of a dead peasant was found to pursue the living, and the inhabitants rushing out to the grave fearfully mutilated the body, to prevent it from committing further injury.

The same conception, from a more charitable point of view, led to the institution of regular meals for the ghosts at stated intervals. In North-eastern India, after the body has been consigned to its final resting-place, a friend of the deceased steps forward, and holding food and drink in his hand, speaks the following suggestive words, "Take and eat: heretofore you have eaten and drunk with us, you can do so no more; you were one of us, you can be so no longer; we come no more to you; come you not to us." In Eastern Africa, the Wanicas are accustomed to fill a cocoa-nut shell with rice and tembo, and place it near the grave. In the Congo district, a channel is dug into the grave leading to the mouth of the corpse, by which means food and drink are duly conveyed. The sense of decorum impels certain Turanian tribes to place not only food, but even napkins, on the graves of their relatives. We cannot resist the temptation of quoting the following passage from Mr. Tylor's graphic account of the manner in which the Chinese feast their ghostly visitors. "Some victuals are left over for any blind or feeble spirit who may be late, and a pail of gruel is provided for headless souls, with spoons for them to put it down their throats with. Such proceedings culminate in the so-called Universal Rescue, now and then celebrated, when a little house is built for the expected visitors, with separate accommodations, and bath rooms for male and female ghosts." * In the Alpach Valley of Tyrol, ghosts released from purgatory on the night of All Souls, return to the houses of the peasantry. A light is left burning in the dining room, and a certain cake, prepared for the occasion, is placed upon the table for their delectation, also a pot of grease for the poor souls to anoint their wounds with.

* Tylor, Primitive Culture, ii, p. 34.

Occasionally, to obviate the necessity of continued attendance upon the dead, a single sumptuous feast is provided immediately after their demise, and this is believed to cancel their claims once for all. In this manner arose the custom of funeral banquets. In England, in the fifteenth century, a noisy revel of three days' duration attended the obsequies of Sir John Paston. The so-called Irish wake originated in the same way. After the first outbreaks of grief have subsided, meat and drink are brought in, chiefly the latter, and what was at first intended for a parting entertainment to the dead, often ends in the boisterous excesses of the living.

It is here proper to remark that the savage tribes who believe in an after existence, do not in many instances claim this privilege for themselves alone, but share it willingly with the lower animals and even with inanimate objects. Weapons, utensils, and even victuals—have their ghostly representatives like men. When a great chief dies, his widow is often forced by public opinion to follow him to the grave, in order that the departed brave may not be wifeless in the hereafter. But besides the widow, his horse, his war-club, his girdle, his favorite trinkets are buried or burned with him to serve his use or vanity in spectre-land.

From what has preceded, it must be clear that

the savage's conception of a ghost bears but a faint and distant resemblance to the idea of soul, as it became current in the schools of philosophy; nor can the latter derive support from the ignorant reasonings, the hasty inductions of primitive man. On the lower levels of culture the idea of immortality indeed is quite unknown. If the ghost continues its shadowy existence after death, it is none the less liable to come to an abrupt end, and then nothing whatever of its former substance remains; it is a pale, filmy thing, exposed to the inroads of the hostile elements, surrounded by numerous dangers, to which it may at any moment succumb. In the Tonga Islands only the souls of the well-born are supposed to survive at all. The common people have no souls worth speaking of, and when they die, are completely extinguished. The ghosts of Guinea negroes are compelled to approach the bank of the terrible river of death. Some of them are thereupon wafted across to lead pleasant lives on the opposite side, others are drowned in the stream, or beaten to atoms with a club. With the Fijians it is always a matter of doubt whether a soul will succeed at all in maintaining its feeble existence after it has left its protecting house of sinew and bone. But they open a peculiarly dismal prospect to wifeless souls. Nanananga, a fierce demoniac being, watches for them on the shore as they approach, and dashes them to pieces upon the rocks. The Greenlanders affirm that after death the soul enters upon a long, lone journey over a mountain full of precipitous descents, covered with ice and snow. The storms howl about its path, and every step is fraught with pain and danger. If any harm happens to the poor wanderer here, then it dies " the other death " from which there is no re-awakening.

In the theories of a future state, as devised by the lower races, we are at a loss to detect the germs of any more spiritual longings. Far from looking forward with pleased anticipation or confidence to the world to come, the barbarian shuddered as he thought of his approaching end, and was loath to exchange the white and sunny world for the dreary companionship of luckless shades. The life that awaited him was not in the majority of instances a better or a higher life than this; not free from the limitations of sense; no larger perfecting of what is here dwarfed and crippled; it was lower, poorer, meaner; it was to the present, what the pressed flower is to the full-blown rose; the same in substance, indeed, but with its beauty perished, and its joyous fragrance evanesced.

The argument from the common consent of mankind in truth deserves no serious attention.*

---

* The doctrine of spiritual immortality is not common to the human race. The material life of the ghost bears no analogy to what we

The argument cannot be substantiated, it would prove nothing, if it could. The general concurrence of the whole human race in any form of error would not make that error less erroneous, and the testimony of united millions against a solitary thinker might kick the beam when balanced in the scales of truth.

When we behold an ignorant knave squandering his ill-gotten gains on superfluities, while honest people are famishing for want of the necessaries; when we see the unscrupulous politician outstripping the deserving statesman, in the race for fame and station; when modest merit shrinks in corners, and the native royalty of talent plays courtier to the kings of lucre, we are reminded of the complaint of Job, that the bad prosper, and the righteous are down-trodden, yet that they sleep together in the dust and the worm covers them alike.

This evident disparity between virtue and happiness has led men to take refuge in the thought of compensation hereafter, and the necessity of a future state in which the good shall be rewarded, and the evil punished, according to the verdict of a just judge, has been deduced even from the apparent injustice of the present. Thus the very imper-

mean by the soul's continuance. The continuance of the ghost's existence is not an immortal continuance.

fections of our own life on earth, afford a pretext for the most ambitious conceptions of human destiny.

The argument from the necessity of reward and punishment is extremely popular among the uneducated, since it appeals ostensibly to their sense of justice and assures them that by the aid of Divine omnipotence, a full correspondence between worthiness and happiness, though vainly expected here, will be established in another sphere. It behooves us to enquire whether there is anything in the nature of virtue, that demands a correspondence of this kind.

The philosopher Epicurus was perhaps the first among the ancients to take strong ground in favor of the utilitarian view of virtue. Pleasure, he holds, is the purpose of existence, and virtue is thus reduced to enlightened self-interest. There are different kinds of pleasure; pleasures of the senses and of the soul. Epicurus points out that the former cannot be considered true pleasures, since they defeat their own end, blunting the capacity of enjoyment in proportion as they are indulged, and incapable of affording permanent satisfaction. Himself a man of refined tastes and fastidious habits, he shrank from the very coarseness of the passions, and counselled moderation, friendship and benevolence. But he refused to recognize in these virtues any intrinsic value of their own, and lauded them only because in contrast to the lower appetites, the enjoyment they afford is lasting and constantly increases with their exercise. It is easy to perceive that when the moral law is thus stripped of its authority to command, the choice between duty and inclination will be governed by fortuitous preferences, and not by principle. It then remains for each individual to decide what form of pleasure may be most congenial to his temper and desires. The philosopher will value the delights of contemplative ease, and of kindly communion with his fellow-men; the passionate youth may hold that a single deep draught from the chalice of sensual pleasure is worth more than a whole lifetime of neutral self-restraint; "eat and drink" will be his motto; "remote consequences—who knows? To-morrow we may die."

Moreover the doctrine of enlightened self-interest has this fatal objection to it, that if consistently applied, at least among the powerful of the earth, it would lead to consequences the very reverse of moral. It is but too true that honesty is not always the best policy; that fraud and violence, when perpetrated on a scale of sufficient magnitude, (instance the division of unfortunate Poland,) are not always punished as they deserve to be. Far from teaching the tyrant to subdue his baser instincts, enlightened self-interest might rather lead him to stifle the accusing voice of conscience, and to root out the scruples that interfere with his ambition. Unless we concede that the moral law has a claim upon us which the constitution of our nature does not permit us to deny with impunity, and that its pleasures differ, not only in degree, but in kind, from all others, virtue, while a necessity to the weak, becomes folly in the strong; and Napoleon, that gigantic egotist, was correct, when he called love a silly infatuation, and sentiment a thing for women.

The principles of Epicurus not only adulterate the motives of goodness with the desire of reward, but they make the reward of desire the very sanction of all virtue, and thus deprive human nature of its best title to nobility.

Truly disinterestedness is the distinguishing mark of every high endeavor. The pursuit of the artist is unselfish, the beauty he creates is his reward. The toil of the scientist in the pursuit of abstract truth is unselfish, the truth he sees is his reward. Why should we hesitate to acknowledge in the domain of ethics, what we concede in the realm of art and science? To say that unselfishness itself is only the more refined expression of a selfish instinct, is to use the term selfish with a double meaning, is a mere empty play on words. We have the innate need of harmony in the moral relations ; this is our glory, and the stamp of the Divine upon our nature. We cannot demonstrate the existence of disinterested motives, any more than we can demonstrate that there is joy in the sunlight and freedom in the mountain breeze. The fact that we *demand unselfishness* in action alone assures us that the standard of enlightened self-interest is false.

And indeed if we consult the opinions of men, where they are least likely to be warped by sophistry, we shall find that disinterestedness is the universal criterion by which moral worth is measured. If we suspect the motive we condemn the act. If a person gives largely for some object of public usefulness or charity, we do not permit the munificence of the gift to deceive our judgment. Perhaps he is merely desirous of vaunting his wealth, perhaps it is social standing he aims at, perhaps he is covetous of fame. If these suspicions prove well founded, the very men who accept his bounty will in their secret hearts despise him, and by a certain revulsion of feeling we shall resent his action all the more, because, not only is he destitute of honorable purpose, but he has filched the fair front of virtue, and defiled the laurel even in the wearing of it.

We do not even accord the name of goodness to that easy, amiable sympathy which leads us to alleviate the sufferings of others, unless it be guided by wise regard for their permanent welfare

The tattered clothes, the haggard looks, the piteous pleading voice of the pauper on the public highway may awaken our pity, but the system of indiscriminate alms-giving is justly condemned as a weakness rather than a virtue.

On the other hand obedience to duty, when it involves pain and self-abnegation, seems to rise in the general estimation. Clearly because in this instance even the suspicion of interested motives is removed, since hardship, injury in estate and happiness, and even the possible loss of life, are among the foreseen consequences of the act. It is for this reason that the Book of Martyrs has become the golden book of mankind, and that the story of their lives never fails to fill us with mingled sorrow, and admiration, and pride. They are monuments on the field of history, milestones on the path of human progress. We regard them and gain new courage and confidence in our better selves. The blazing pyre on the Campo Fiore, whereon Giordano Bruno breathes his last, becomes a beacon-light for the truth-seeker; the dying Socrates still pours benignant peace over many a sufferer's couch; the Man of sorrows, on Calvary, comforts the hearts of the Christian millions. In the presence of these high examples the inadequacy of the selfish standard becomes clearly apparent. We recognize what a sublime quality that is in man which enables him, not only to triumph over torment and suffering, but to devote his very self to destruction for the sake of honor and truth. Freely must virtue be wooed, not for the dowry she may bring; by loyal devotion to her for her own sake only, can she be won!

If thus it appears that not only is there nothing in the nature of virtue to warrant a claim to reward, but that it is her very nature to disclaim any reward, it will become plain that the problem, as stated in the beginning, rests upon an entirely false foundation. That the unrighteous and unprincipled should enjoy temporal happiness, does not offend the law of justice. That you, my good sir, honest in all your dealings, truthful in all your acts, should be unhappy, is greatly to be deplored. Why evil and unhappiness should have been allowed at all to enter a world created by an all good and all powerful Being may fairly be asked. Why those who possess the treasure of a clear conscience should not also possess the lesser goods of earth, is a question with which morality is in no wise concerned.

Virtue can have no recompense, save as it is its own recompense, and vice can receive no real punishment save as it is its own avenger. The hope of immortality, in so far as it is based upon the supposed necessity of righting in a future state what is here wrong, is therefore untenable, for it is based upon the assumption of a wrong which exists in the imagination merely. *And he who claims a reward because of his virtue, has thereby forfeited his right to maintain the claim, since that is not virtue, which looks for reward.*

Having endeavored to show that the joys of earth cannot be claimed as the recompense of a moral life, we must yet admit that the desire of happiness is altogether too strong and deep-seated in human nature to be thus summarily dismissed. We seek happiness on its own account quite apart from any title which virtue may give us to its enjoyment. Were we created for misery? Does not the poverty and general unsatisfactoriness of our present condition warrant us in expecting ampler fulfilment, permanent bliss in an after life? I think we shall derive some assistance in discussing this question, by attempting to resolve the conception of happiness into its constituent elements.

Pleasure has been defined to consist in the satisfaction of any of man's natural wants. The variety of our pleasures corresponds to the diversity of our wants.

Food to the hungry, rest to the weary, are sources of pleasure. To feel on some cold wintry day the genial warmth of the hearth fire creeping into our blood, and the frozen limbs relaxing their stiffness, is pleasure. All men admire the beautiful and delight in adornment. Even the rude savage seeks to gratify his æsthetic tastes, so far as the means which nature places at his command permit. The custom of tattooing the skin is widely practiced among the lower races, and stars and circles, trees and plants, and other ingenious devices are impressed with laborious patience upon the different members of the body. The chiefs of the Fiji Islanders, a nude and cannibal race, are represented as wearing an elaborate head-dress of three and even five feet in dimensions, and were accustomed to spend several hours each day, under the care of the royal hair-dresser. Among civilized men the desire for adornment finds vent chiefly in external objects, while every coarse solicitation of attention to the person is shunned. Tastily decorated houses, flowers, paintings, music, gratify our sense of symmetry, and spread an atmosphere of culture and refinement in the vicinity of our daily occupations.

But there are deeper and purer joys in reserve. Man is eminently a social being; he has the need of sympathy and depends upon the affections of his fellows. The presence of cherished companions and friends becomes a necessity to him; in absence he yearns for it, and the lack of it is one of the most serious afflictions of human life. "Woe unto him who, far from parents and loved kinsmen, a lonely life must lead. His present joys devouring grief doth snatch. His thoughts are ever straying in the distance back to his father's hall, where the sun of life first rose upon him, and where children of the common home, playfully, with gentle bonds, close and closer drew their hearts together."* The tranquil delight which we derive from the enlargement of intellect, and the exquisite inward satisfaction that results from high fidelity to duty, may be mentioned as the last to crown the scale of pleasures.

Now, it is evident that all these elements of happiness, these diverse rays that nowhere melt into the perfect light, are dependent upon the physical organization of man, such as it is, even for their partial attainment; of the lower pleasures, this is at once evident. But a little reflection will show the same to be the case with the higher. If we consider the æsthetic faculty, we find its gratification conditioned by a physical basis. What were music without the ear; what the symmetry of form, without the eye and touch? The intellect, in its turn, fashions the rough timber of experience, which an ever flowing stream of sensation carries into the workshop of the brain. Can the mind feed upon itself? Can the laws of thought act otherwise

* Goethe, Iphigenie auf Tauris, Act I.

than upon the material afforded by the senses? The same is also true with respect to our moral qualities, and the exercise of the virtues is inconceivable beyond the pale of human society. All virtue presupposes a tendency to err; the failings and limitations of our mortal condition. Justice is the adjustment of limitations common to all men in such manner that their stress shall not bear more heavily upon one than upon the other. Love is the expansion of one limited nature in another and their mutual enrichment by such union. Charity, fortitude, continence, whatever we applaud in human conduct, is but an indirect testimony to the natural imperfections inherent in the human heart, and is accounted admirable only in so far as it tends to ensure the best interests of the race on earth. When therefore this body is corrupted, when we depart from out the fellowship of men, the gratification of the appetites, the enjoyment of beauty, the exercise of reason, and the practice of virtue become alike unthinkable.

We desire larger happiness than we can here achieve; but because we desire a thing, are we therefore at all warranted in believing that we shall obtain it? Is the course of the world's affairs such as to encourage so flattering an hypothesis? Is not the fatality that so often attends our best efforts in this life, an argument against, rather than

IMMORTALITY. 23

in favor of increasing felicity in another? We should assume a wiser attitude as against fate. There are those who fret under disappointment, and murmur and rebel as if they had been defrauded of a right ; as if they had entered into a compact with destiny to their advantage, as if the myriad worlds moved through space for their especial good. This is an insane spirit. We need something of the vim of stoicism to grapple with the difficulties of life ; we need to cultivate a larger patience; an humble spirit prepared for every loss, and welcoming every hour of joy as an unlooked for gain. There are a thousand pleasures too in little things which we, with the petulance of children, daily spurn, because we cannot have all we ask for. In every stone there is instruction, in every varying aspect of the sky there is beauty, wherever men congregate and commune, lessons of wisdom are revealed to the observer. The movement of everlasting laws quivers in the meanest trifles, and the eternities, thinly veiled, look out upon us with their solemn gaze from every passing mask of time. These let us study; art will help us; science will open to us a wondrous chain of workings which the mind cannot exhaust, and active exertions for the common weal will give a generous glow to our lives, and still the unquiet yearnings which we may never entirely set at rest. You have seen how the flowers grow, how that many seeds are scattered and but few take root; how the germ slowly and with difficulty develops. The rain waters it. the warm sunbeam fosters it; storms sweeping over the earth, may crush it while it is still a young and tender shoot. At last, sometimes after years of preparation, it buds and opens and blooms and becomes a delight and a glory, a fount of fragrance, a crown of beauty. A few days pass and it droops; what the long process of time has slowly created, a single moment may suffice to destroy; and yet though its time was brief, the flower fulfilled its nature only in that passing bloom; all the previous stages of its existence had a meaning only as they led up to this, the final revelation of its purpose.

The bloom of human life is morality; whatever else we may possess, health, and wealth, power, grace, knowledge, have a value only as they lead up to this; have a meaning only as they make this possible. Nor should we complain that the blight of death so quickly withers what the course of three-score years has scarce sufficed to produce. In the hour of our destruction, we will lift up our hearts in triumph—we have blossomed! We have blossomed!

But it will be said, that the flower when it is wilted and withered here, may be transplanted to fairer regions; that the soul may take on new organs, when it has abandoned its earthly habitation, and in a series of transformations of which, it is true, we can form no definite conception, may enter afresh upon its struggles for worthiness in other spheres. This is, indeed, the loftiest expression which the hope of immortality has found. Unlike the arguments previously considered, it is unalloyed by any selfish motive, is founded upon a really exalted sentiment, and it is Love and Virtue themselves that here take up the strain, and sing us their animating song of ceaseless progress toward the good. The argument in this shape, involves the further question whether the existence of an independent and indestructible soul is assured, and upon this point the whole problem of immortality finally hinges.

The question whether what we are accustomed to call the soul is a distinct and indivisible entity, or merely the result of material processes, has divided mankind for more than two thousand years, and some of the ablest thinkers have ranged themselves on either side. As early as the fifth century B. C. the philosopher Democritus propounded materialistic doctrines among the Greeks. According to him, the soul is a combination of smooth, round, polished and moving atoms, and to the motions of these atoms the phenomena of life are to be ascribed.

Among the Romans, Lucretius advanced similar views. He took particular pains to combat the "vulgar fear of death," protesting that the prospect of dissolution would lose its terrors, did we not foolishly imagine ourselves conscious of being dead, forgetting that death implies the entire cessation of consciousness. The followers of materialistic opinions among the ancients, were not a few. But during the ascendancy of the Christian Church, these opinions retired into the background, until in the seventeenth and eighteenth centuries, they were revived by such men as Gassendi and La Mettrie, and others. In modern times they have been widely spread.

The list of names on the opposite side is headed by Socrates, Plato, Aristotle, and embraces the great majority of writers and public teachers, down to the present day.

It may appear strange that when the belief in immortality had once become current, men should have been tempted to forego its pleasing prospects, and even, with a certain vehemence, to urge their sceptical views upon others. Let us consider for a moment, what it was that induced the materialists to assume their position. The observed correspondence between mental and physical phenomena doubtless led them in the first instance to adopt their peculiar views.

We see in the tiny body of the new born babe,

barely more than the faint stirrings of animal life; months pass by before it is able to form any clear conception of the persons and things in its vicinity, the simpler mental processes appearing simultaneously with the growth of the bodily organs. The intellect reaches its highest development in the age of manhood and womanhood, when we stand in the maturity of our physical powers. In that middle age of life lies, with rare exceptions, the best work we are destined to accomplish. Having entered upon the downward slope, our faculties gradually lose their vigor, until we sink into the final stage of drivelling old age, and become feeble in mind, as we are helpless in body. In this manner the close connection between our spiritual and material parts, is brought home forcibly, even to the unreflecting; as the one enlarges so does the other: as the one diminishes so does the other: together they increase, together they are weakened; the inference is drawn, shall it not be, that together they will perish?

The phenomena of sleep and of coma seem to convey the same lesson. A haze steals over our consciousness; sometimes settling into impenetrable night; as the body for a time wears the semblance of death, so also is the mind stupefied or completely paralyzed. Hours pass by; in the interval, the business of the world has gone on as before, but to us there has been only a void and utter blank. And thus it is said shall there be a void and a blank in the tomb; time will pass by, and we shall not know it; men will move and act and we shall be none the wiser for it; it will be all like sleep, only that there will be no dreams.

And again when some malignant fever seizes upon the body and corrupts the currents of the blood, how do the poor disordered thoughts dance about wildly, driven by the lash of the distemper; how does the use of stimulants besot the intellect, so that every higher power is deadened; how in the wild ravings of the diseased brain, do we behold the hideous mockery of mind.

And does not the grave itself testify loudly that the end is an end indeed; the body falls to pieces, the dust commingles with the dust, and nothing remains, nothing at least of which we can ever have experience. Right or wrong, these facts impress the mind, and their leaden weight serves to drag down our aspirations.

It is true, the considerations I have enumerated are based upon a mere surface view of things, but the more accurate methods of science seem, at first sight, to confirm the general conclusions to which they lead. On this point, it would be well to dwell for a moment. John Stuart Mill acknowledges that "the evidence is well-nigh complete that all thought and feeling has some action of the bodily organism for its immediate coincident and accompaniment, and that the specific variations, and especially the different degrees of complication of the nervous and cerebral organism, correspond to differences in the development of our mental faculties."

The prodigious difficulties in the way of the study of the brain may long retard the progress of the investigator, but for the purposes of our argument we are at liberty to assume whatever is within the limits of possible achievement. We may suppose that physiology will succeed so far that the brain will be accurately and completely mapped out, and that the motions of the atoms upon which the thousand varying modes of thought and feeling depend, will be known and measured. In anticipating such results, we have reached the utmost tenable position of materialism.

But now to our surprise we discover that all this being allowed, the ultimate question, what is soul, remains still unsolved and as insoluble as ever. The unvarying coincidence of certain modes of soul with certain material processes may be within the range of proof, but what cannot be proven is, that these material processes explain the psychic phenomena.

If it is urged that the same difficulty presents itself in the explanation of the most ordinary occurrences, this objection is based upon a misapprehension of the point at issue.

The scientist cannot show why heat should be convertible into motion, but how it is thus transformed is easy to demonstrate, and the exact mechanical equivalent of heat has been calculated. But how certain motions of atoms in the brain should generate, not heat, but consciousness, but thought and love, is past all conception. There are here two different orders of facts, having no common principle to which they could both be reduced. There is an impassable gulf between them which can in nowise be bridged over.

Nor would it avail us to endow the atom itself with the promise and potency of intellect; we should thereby throw back the issue a step further, and disguise the problem whose existence it were better to plainly acknowledge. The broad fact of consciousness therefore remains unexplained and inexplicable as before. Arrived at this limit, science itself pauses and refuses to pass further.

Some of the leading naturalists of our day have lately expressed themselves clearly and tersely in this sense. The eminent physiologist Dubois Reymond denies that the connection between certain motions of certain atoms in the brain, and what he calls, the primal, undefinable and undeniable facts of consciousness, is at all conceivable. Professor Tyndall in his address on "The scope and limits of Scientific Materialism," explains his views with similar precision. Were our minds so expanded, strengthened and illuminated as to enable us to see and feel the very molecules of the brain; were we capable of following all their motions, all their groupings, all their electric discharges, if such there be; and were we intimately acquainted with the corresponding states of thought and feeling, we should be as far as ever from the solution of the problem. How are these physical processes connected by and with the facts of consciousness? I do not think the materialist is entitled to say that his molecular groupings and his molecular motions explain everything, in reality they explain nothing. . . The problem of body and soul is as insoluble in its modern form as it was in the pre-scientific ages."

Now since it is impossible to demonstrate that the powers of mind are a product of matter, the possibility undoubtedly remains that these powers may continue to exist even after their connection with the physical organism has been dissolved. If all the arguments that are commonly adduced in support of the doctrine of a future life fall short of their object, it is but just to add that every argument to the contrary is equally devoid of foundation. The doctrine of immortality cannot be disproved. Of the nature of soul we are in absolute ignorance; we know nothing; what is more, we can know nothing. At this point we touch the utmost boundary of human reason, and must be content to write mystery of mysteries.

In the state of settled uncertainty to which we are thus reduced, the shape of our opinions will be determined by the bias of our natures or the influence of education. The sceptic will remind us of the points in which we resemble all the perishable forms of nature and hold it improbable that we alone should escape the universal law of dissolution. Others will cling to the hope of continued life, even on the brink of the grave, and the strong instinct of self preservation will give tone and color to their religious beliefs. Deep philosophical speculations are possible as to that ultimate source of being, that hidden light of which both matter and mind are diverse reflections. And here too poetry assumes its legitimate office. On the mists that cover the infinite abyss, we may project whatever images, foul or fair, we list. Science you may be sure will never disturb us. Dogmatic assertion however, on either side is totally unwarranted: and the question of immortality (I think we must sooner or later make up our minds to that) will remain an open one. Certain, only, is the fact of our uncertainty.

If the conclusions to which we have thus been led, seem purely negative in their bearings, they are none the less capable of certain positive applications, which deserve our serious attention. The longing for immortality has been developed into a morbid craving under the influence of the current religious teachings, and has become a disturbing element in human society. On more than one occasion it has imperilled the peace of nations, and the doctrines of salvation became the watchwords of contending armies. The doubtful chances of eternal felicity or damnation became the one absorbing topic on which men's minds dwelt, and the wild horrors of the Christian Hell have cast a gloom over many an innocent life, and curtailed the scant measure of its earthly happiness. It were something gained, if by a cool and dispassionate judgment the influence of these dismal fantasies could be lessened, and men be freed from their slavish subjection to phantoms born of their own distempered imaginations.

Furthermore, it follows from what we have said that the belief in immortality should not be inculcated as a dogma in our schools of religion, and above all that the dictates of the moral law should in no wise be made to depend upon it for their sanction. The moral law is the common ground upon which all religious and in fact all true men may meet. It is the one basis of union that remains to us amid the clashing antagonisms of the sects. While dogma is by its nature, open to attack, and its acceptance at all times a matter of choice, the principles of morality have a right to demand implicit obedience, and should rest as everlasting verities in the human heart. Let us reflect well before we imperil the latter by the undue prominence which we give the former. It is not needful to impart to a child the whole truth, but what it learns should be wholly true, and nothing should be taught it as a fundamental fact which it can ever in after years be led to call in question. How often has it occurred that when the riper reason of the man has rejected the tenets of the church in which he was educated, he has been tempted to cast aside all the religious teachings of his youth, the moral with the rest, as idle fable and deceit.

And lastly, friends, as we do not, cannot know, it is presumably wise that we should not know. The vanity of all our efforts to grasp the infinite, should teach us that on this island of time whereon we live, lies our work. In its joys we may freely take delight; for its woes we should reserve our sympathies, and in laboring to advance the progress of the good we must find our satisfaction.

Before closing this subject however let us recall vividly to our minds that the desire for continuance after death is capable of the most noble expression, and of supplying us with wholesome consolation and inspiriting motives to action. The individual passes, but the race lives! There is a law in nature that no force is ever lost. The thousand varying forms that ebb and flow around us are various only to our feeble vision. At the core they are one, transmuted, yet the same, changing yet changeless, perishing to rise anew. The law of the conservation of energy holds good throughout the entire domain of matter. And such a law too obtains in our spiritual life. The law of the conservation of moral energy is no less an abiding truth; we are not dust merely, that returns to dust; we are not summer flies that bask in the sunshine of the passing day; we are not bounded in our influence by the narrow tenure of our years. Say not when the sod has closed above those who have been dear to you that all is gone. Say not that the grace and loveliness, and wisdom that once dwelt within the pallid form is breathed away like a hollow wind. Nor yet stand idly gazing upon the cloud-land of the future, watching if you can trace perchance their shadowy lineaments fading into the dimness of untried worlds. The dead are not dead if we have loved them truly. In our own lives we give them immortality. Let us arise and take up the work they have left unfinished, and preserve the treasures they have won, and round out the circuit of their being to the fullness of an ampler orbit in our own.

All the good that was in them lives in you, the

germ and nucleus of the better that shall be. All the evil that inhered in them shall be cleansed away in you and your virtues shall be the atonement for their sins. Thus shall the fathers live in the children, and from generation to generation the bond that connects the past with the future remains unbroken. They that have left you are not afar; their presence is near and real, a silent and august companionship. In the still hours of meditation; under the starlit night, in the stress of action, in trials and temptations, you will hear their voices whispering words of cheer or warning, and your deeds are their deeds and your lives are their lives.

So does the light of other days still shine in the bright hued flowers that clothe our fields; so do they who are long since gathered into the silent city of the dead still move about our houses, distributing kindness and nobleness among our lives. So does the toll of the funeral bell become an alarum to rouse us to more active effort and to the nobler service of mankind.

II.

RELIGION.

THE question, Have we still a religion, propounded by David Friedrich Strauss some few years ago, will long engage the attention of radical thinkers. It is clear that to answer it satisfactorily we must determine, in the first instance, what meaning ought rightly to be attached to the term religion. In common parlance, it is often used with reference to mere externals, a religious person being one who conforms to the rites and usages of some particular church. On the other hand, every innovation in the sphere of doctrine is branded as irreligious. Thus Luther was deemed irreligious by the Catholics; St. Boniface by the heathen Germans, Jesus by the Jews, Elijah by the servants of Baal. There is not any single form, nor even a single fundamental principle common to all religions. Religion is not identical with theology. It is indeed often maintained that the belief in a personal God should be regarded as the foundation and criterion of religion; but upon this assumption, two facts remain inexplicable, the existence of religion before ever the idea of a deity had arisen among men, and the existence of what may be termed an atheistical religion, in conscious antagonism to the doctrine of a personal God. Among the lower races we find men worshipping, sacrificing and uttering their invocations to mountains, fountains, rivers, rocks and stones: they know not a deity—sometimes they have not even idols, and yet they certainly have, after a fashion of their own, a religion. Again, Buddhism, while possessing a subtle system of philosophy and an admirable code of ethics, starts with the proposition that there never was a creation, and in consequence, never a creator, and yet more than four hundred millions of the earth's inhabitants call it their religion!

The question returns to us, What is religion? It is not creed; it is not sacrifice; it is not prayer; it is not covered by the dogmas of any special form of belief; it has acted as a controlling force in all ages, in every zone, among all manner of men. Are we devoid of it? Of it? Of what?

The feeling which the presence of the Infinite in the thoughts of man awakens within him, is called, the feeling of the sublime. *The feeling of the sublime is the root of the religious sentiment.* It assumes various phases, and to these correspond the various religions. Let us endeavor to enumerate some of the most prominent.

The feeling of the sublime is awakened by the mysterious. The indefinite gives us our earliest presentiment of the infinite; the religion of mystery is fetishism. The feeling of the sublime is awakened by exhibitions of superhuman power. The religion of power is paganism. The feeling of the sublime is evoked by vastness; the religions of vastness are Brahminism and Buddhism. The loftiest type of sublimity is to be found in the morally infinite. Judaism, Christianity and Islam have sought to give it expression.*

Let us discuss in the first place the origin of Fetishism. There are certain natural phenomena that fill us with alarm, without our being able to attribute the effect to any definite cause. The darkness of night, the rustling of leaves, the moaning of the wind through the forest, the wailing cry of certain birds, and the peculiar effects of a gathering fog, are of this kind. I have had occasion to observe a little child suddenly starting from its play with every sign of fear depicted upon its countenance; the spasm passed away as quickly as it had come, but was repeated at various intervals, until at last the child ran up to me in uncontrollable alarm,

* We do not pretend that the above schedule is at all exhaustive. Various elements of the sublime, not mentioned in the text, have entered into the composition of each of the great religions. We have merely attempted to seize the more salient feature of a few leading types.

and threw up its arms for protection: it was a raw wintry day, a gusty wind blew fitfully against the windows; and the dreary sound of the rattling panes could be distinctly heard in the stillness of the room; on closer observation I noticed that the signs of alarm in the child recurred with great regularity, as often as this sound was repeated. In a similar way we may imagine our earliest ancestors to have been affected by whatever was vague and mysterious in nature. The sense of uncertainty occasioned in this manner, gave rise in the primitive man to the first conceptions of mysterious powers beyond him.

The invention, or rather the discovery, of fire tended still further in the same direction. To us it is barely possible to imagine life without this most useful of the elements. The wild beast flees fire and fears it, man uses it, and it becomes the chief instrument of civilization. But if we strive to picture to ourselves the state of the savage's mind on his first acquaintance with fire and its properties we shall find him utterly at a loss to account for. How will he regard this nimble, playful being, so bright and yet so fearful in its ravages. Of the laws of chemical action he has of course no conception, but he has sometimes seen the lightning strike into the wood of the tree, and now from the same wood he evokes the semblance of the lightning. He is twirling two dry sticks between his hands; of a sudden, a lambent flame shoots forth, seizes the wood, makes away with it, and leaves nothing but blackened cinders behind. Whence did it come, whither has it vanished? Here was a new mystery; a spiritual presence, latent in trees and stones; kindly and beneficent at times, then again hostile and fiercely destructive.

The mystery of the preparation of fire is celebrated in the ancient hymns of the Vedah. We there find its birth from the friction of the double sticks described, and its properties rehearsed in reverent language. It is invoked like any superior spirit to bless its votaries, and to protect them from harm. The important role ascribed to fire in the sacred usages of the ancients, is well-known, and the origin of fire worship apparent.

The theory of dreams, to which we have referred on a previous occasion, contributed in like manner, to extend the boundaries of the world of mystery. Convinced that he bore within himself an airy counterfeit of self, the savage attributed the same species of possession to things animate and inanimate alike. Why should not beasts and rivers and stones have their ghosts like man? Moreover, as to the ghosts of the human dead, no one could tell where they might take up their abode. They might be anywhere and everywhere. Their countless legions surrounded the living in all places. They were heard shouting in the echo among the hills; they were seen to ride past on the midnight gale. Often they assumed the shape of birds and reptiles and beasts of prey. Those creatures were singled out with a preference, whose movements and habits suggested the idea of mystery. Thus the owl was supposed to harbor an evil spirit, and the serpent was worshipped because of its stealthy, gliding motion, its venomous bite, and the fascination in its eye. Serpent worship existed the world over. Traces of it are preserved in the literature of the Greeks and Romans, and it was practised even among the Hebrews, as the Books of Kings attest. Among certain African tribes it is still customary to keep huge serpents in temples, and priests are dedicated to their service. Powerful animals also, such as the bear, the lion and the tiger, were sometimes supposed to contain the ghosts of departed chieftains, and were revered accordingly.

If we remember the unfriendly relations supposed to subsist between the living and the dead, we may conceive the state of alarm in which our primitive ancestors must have passed their lives on beholding themselves thus beset on every side, with ghosts or demons in disguise. A thousand fabulous terrors haunted their imagination. Wherever they turned they suspected lurking foes;

spirits were in the earth, in the air, in birds, in animals, in reptiles, in trees. They could not move a step without infringing on the boundaries of the spirit realm. Every object the least extraordinary in size, or shape, or color, appeared to them the token of some demon's presence, and was worshipped in consequence, not on its own account, but because of the mystery which it suggested.

In this manner Fetishism arose. The fetish worshipper leaves his hut in the morning, sees some bright pebble glistening on his path, lifts it from the ground and says, this shall be my fetish. If he succeeds in the business of the day, he places the little object in a shrine, gilds it, brings it food, addresses his prayers to it; if it fails, it is cast aside. Again, if after a little time the fetish ceases to fulfil his wishes, he breaks it and drags it in the mire by way of punishment.

Such are a few of the gross and grotesque conceptions to which the religion of mystery has given birth. It is true, to the educated mind of the present day they will appear the very reverse of sublime. But greatness is relative, and our own loftier conceptions of the sublime are but the slow result of a long process of growth and development.

THE RELIGION OF POWER.—It has often been said that fear is the beginning of religion; a statement of this kind however, cannot be accepted, without serious qualification. There is a sense of kinship with the great, in whatever form it may appear, of which even the meanest are susceptible. A nation worships the hero who ruins it; and slaves will take a certain pride in the superiority of their masters. It is not fear so much as admiration of might which makes men servants of the mighty. The first tyrants on earth were, in all likelihood, strong, agile, and brave men, possessing in an extraordinary degree, the qualities which all others coveted. They won applause, they were looked up to as natural leaders, and the arm of force maintained what the esteem of their fellows had accorded in the first instance. There is a touch of the sublime even in the rudest adoration of force.

In the second stage of religious development, which we are now approaching, the theory of possession discussed in the above, was extended to the heavenly bodies, and the sun, moon and stars were endowed with the attributes of personal beings. Hence the origin of the great gods. As the sun is the most conspicuous body in the heavens, the sun god figures as the central deity in every pantheon. The various phases through which the luminary passes are represented in distinct personalities. We find gods of the rising sun and of the setting sun; gods of the sun of spring, summer and winter, gods also of the cloud-enshrouded sun, that battles with the storm giants.

Since the hosts of heaven were supposed to be beings allied in nature to ourselves, the action and interaction of the meteoric phenomena was ascribed to personal motives, and the ingenuity of the primitive philosophers was exhausted in finding plausible pretexts to explain their attractions and repulsions, their seeming friendships and hostilities. Thus arose the quaint and fanciful myths with which the traditions of antiquity abound. Those problems which the modern mind seeks to settle with the help of scientific investigation, the limited experience of an earlier age was barely competent to attack, and it covered with some pretty fiction, the difficulties which it could not solve. The genealogy and biography of the sun-god formed the main theme of all mythologies.

The daily progress of the sun through the heavens, is described as follows: Each morning the golden crowned god leaves his golden palace in the East, deep down below the ocean's waves; he mounts his golden chariot, drawn by fiery steeds. A rosy fingered maiden opens the purple gate of day, upward rush the steeds through blinding mist along the steep ascent of heaven, down they plunge at evening into the cooling waters of the sea; the naiads await the deity and bear him backward to his orient home.

Again the fair youth Adonis is said to come out of the forest, where nymphs had nurtured him. Venus and he hunt in joyous company through wood and dale. One day Adonis is slain; the blood that trickled from his wounds has turned the roses red, and the tender anemones have sprung from the tears that love wept when she beheld his fall. The young god who comes out of the forest is Spring; for a time he disports joyously on earth, with love for his companion, but his term of life is quickly ended. Spring dies, but ever returns anew. Among the Syrian women it was customary for a long period to observe the festival of the Adoneiah; with every sign of grief they first bemoaned the god's untimely death; they beat their breasts, cut off the rich luxuriance of their hair; showed upon his effigy the marks of the wounds he had received; bound him with linen bands, anointed him with costly oil and spices, and then buried him. On the seventh day the cry was heard, Adonis lives, Adonis is resurrected from the grave. The story of a young god typical of the Spring who suffers a premature death, and after a time resurrects from the grave is well known in the mythologies of other nations.

The progress of the sun through the seasons is thus personified. The rays of the sun are described as the locks of the sun-god's hair. When the sun's heat waxes, these locks increase in abundance, when it wanes they diminish, until in mid-winter the head of the sun-god is entirely bald. At this season the god is supposed to be exceedingly weak, and his eye, bright in the summer, is now become blind. He is far from his home, and subject to the power of his enemies, the wintry storms. These traits recur in the familiar Hebrew myth of Samson. The word Samson means sun; he is bound with ropes, as is also the sun-god among the Polynesians. The secret of his strength is in his hair. Shorn of this the giant becomes feeble as a child, and is blinded by his foes.

But it is the sun in its conflict with the demons of the storm, the sun as a warrior and a hero, that chiefly attracts the *religious* reverence of the heroic age. In nature there is no more striking exhibition of power than is revealed in the phenomena of the thunder-storm. Even to us it has not lost its sublimity, and a sense of awe overcomes us whenever the mighty spectacle is enacted in the heavens. Primitive man had a far deeper interest in the issue of the tempest than we are now capable of appreciating. To him the clouds appeared to be ferocious monsters, and when they crowded about the central luminary, he feared that they might quench its light in everlasting darkness. The very existence of the universe seemed to be threatened. The sun-god, the true friend of man, however arises to wage war against the demons: a terrific uproar follows and the contending forces meet. Do you hear Thor's far-sounding hammer, Jove's bolt falling in the thunder clap: do you see Indra's lightning-spear flashing across the sky, and piercing the sides of the storm dragon? The light triumphs; the tempest rolls away, but presently returns to be again defeated. In this way arose the transparent stories of Jupiter's conflict with Typhon, his precipitate flight, and his final victory; the story of Indra's warfare against the writhing serpent, Vritra, and numerous others that might be mentioned. It is the sun-god who flashes the lightning and hurls the thunder. To him men owe the maintenance of the order of existence. He is the mightiest of the gods. Fighting their battles on high, he is invoked by the warriors to aid them in their earthly conflicts; he takes precedence of all the other deities; he the strongest god is raised to the throne of the celestial state.

Now if we study the history of these deities, their intercourse among themselves and with men, we find them to be no more than colossal images of ourselves cast on the mists of the unknown. It is our face and form that Jupiter wears; the echo of our wishes comes back to us in his oracles. "If horses and cows could draw their gods," an ancient philosopher has pointedly said, "as horses and cows would they draw them." The gods share our passions, the good and the evil, distinguished only in this, that what we feebly attempt, they can execute on a scale of gigantic magnitude. They love and bless and shower a thousand gifts upon their worshippers; but they can hate also; are vain, vindictive, cruel.

The gods demand tribute. Like the kings of earth, they received the best share of the spoils of war and of the chase; and gold and silver also was deposited in their sanctuaries. Perfumed incense and dainty cakes were placed upon their altars. The gods are hungry, they must be fed. The gods are thirsty, and certain strong narcotic beverages were brewed especially for their benefit. For this among the Hindoos the juice of the soma plant was mixed with pure milk.

The gods demand blood. The wide prevalence of human sacrifice is the saddest fact that stains the annals of religious history. Among the Fijians the new boat of the chieftain was not permitted to venture upon the waves until it had been washed with human blood, in order to secure it against shipwreck. Among the Khonds of India, we learn that the body of a human victim was literally torn in pieces and his blood mixed with the new turned clod, in order to insure a plentiful harvest. It is estimated that at least twenty-five hundred human beings were annually sacrificed in the temples of Mexico. Human sacrifice was known among the Greeks, and its practice among the Hebrews is recorded in the Hebrew Bible.

When the manners of men ameliorated, and gentler customs began to supplant the barbarous usages of an earlier day, the tyranny of the gods was still feared, but various modes of substitution were adopted to appease their jealousy of human happiness. In India we are told, that the god of light being displeased with the constant effusion of blood, commanded a buffalo to appear from out the jungle, and a voice was heard saying, sacrifice the buffalo and liberate the man.

Another mode of substitution was to give a part for the whole. Some one member of the body was mutilated or curtailed in order to indicate that the person's life was in reality forfeit to the god. Among certain of the aboriginal tribes of America, the youth, on reaching the years of maturity, was forced to place his hand upon a buffalo's skull, and one or more joints of the finger were then cut off and dedicated to the great spirit. There were other modes of mutilation of which I dare not speak, but I will briefly add that the so-called rite of the

RELIGION. 51

covenant, which is practised among the Jews even at the present day, rose in exactly the same manner. Of course the original signification of the custom has been forgotten and a purely symbolical meaning has been attached to it. Nevertheless, its continuance is a disgrace to religion. The grounds of sanity on which it is urged, are not in themselves tenable, and if they were, religion would have no concern with them. It is but a fresh instance of the stubborn vitality which seems to inhere in the hoary superstitions of the past.

Occasionally, when a whole people was threatened with destruction, some prominent and beloved individual was selected for sacrifice, in order that by his death he might save the rest. The same feature was also introduced into the legends of the gods. Philo tells us that the great God El whom the Hebrews and Phœnicians worshiped, once descended to earth, and became a king. This El was the supreme deity. He had an only son whom he loved. One day when great dangers threatened his people, the god determined to sacrifice his only begotten ($μονογενης$) son and to redeem his people: and year by year thereafter a solemn festival was celebrated in Phœnicia in honor of that great sacrifice.

The religion of force has left its dark traces in the history of mankind. Even the higher religions accepted, while they spiritualized, its degrading conceptions into their systems. Slowly only and with the general spread of intelligence and morality, can we hope that its last vestiges will be purged from the minds of men.

Vastness is an element of the sublime. In the religious conceptions of the Hindoos we find it illustrated. It entered alike into the system of the Brahmin and of the Buddhist, and determined their tone and quality. A certain fondness for the gigantic, is peculiar to Hindoo character. Witness the almost boundless periods of their ancient chronology; the colossal forms with which the remains of their monuments and architecture abound. A great Aryan nation having advanced from the waters of the Indus to the shores of the sacred Ganges and having subdued the natives by the force of superior numbers or bravery, had learned to forget the active pursuits of war, and yielded to the lassitude engendered by the climate of their new settlements. Around them they beheld a rich and luxuriant vegetation; birds of rare and many colored plumage, stately trees rising from interminable jungles. Ravishing perfumes lulled their senses as they reposed in the shade of these fairy-like forests. It was a land suited to dreamy contemplation. Here the philosophic priests might dwell upon the vastness of the Universal, and the imagination bewildered by the ever shifting phenomena of the scene might well seek some principle of unity which could connect and explain the whole. Brahma was the name they gave to the pervading Spirit of All things. From Brahma the entire order of existence has emanated: the elements of material things, plants, birds, beasts and men. The lower castes came forth first and are nearest the brutes; the castes of free-born workmen, and of warriors next, the priests and saints last, in whom the world's soul found its loftiest expression.

To Brahma all things must return. Passing through an endless series of transformations, and paying in the long and painful interval the penalty of every crime it has committed, the migrating spirit of man is led back at last to its primal source, and is resolved in the Brahma whence it arose. The connection between individual and universal life was thus kept constantly in view. The soul in the course of its wanderings might pass through every conceivable mode of existence; might assume the shape of creeping plants and worms, and wild animals; might rise to the possession of miraculous powers in the heavens of the Rishis, while its final destiny was to be reunited with the One and All.

The Buddhist Nirvana resembles the Brahma in being accounted the ultimate principle of the world. When in the sixth century B. C. the royal Hermit of the Çakyas revolted against the cruel despotism of the priesthood, the legend relates that the sight of suffering in the forms of sickness, old age and death, roused him from a life of indolent pleasure, and impelled him to seek a remedy for the ills of human life. His counsels were sweet and kindly ; he taught self-control and wise moderation in the indulgence of the passions, and brotherly help and sympathy to lessen the evils which foresight cannot avert. He lifted the degraded masses of the Indian land from out their dull despair ; he warred against the distinctions of caste, he took women and slaves for his companions, he was a prophet of the people, whom the people loved. But even to him the ills of this mortal condition seemed little when compared with the endless possibilities of future ill that awaited the soul in the course of its ceaseless transmigrations. He yearned to shorten its weary path to the goal; and the mystic methods by which he sought to enter Nirvana were a means adapted to this end. Nirvana is the beginning and the end of things. Nirvana in which there is neither action nor feeling; in which intelligence and consciousness are submerged, appeared to this pessimist preacher the last, the only reality. Life is a delusion, real only in its pains: the entire cossation of conscious existence, is the solution he offers to human suffering.

Nirvana is the universal—its conception is vast and dim; it hovers in the distance before the pilgrim of the earth; there will he find rest.

Unlike the Western nations, the Hindoos regarded the idea of immortality with dread and terror, rather than pleased anticipation. The highest promises of their religion, were intended to assure them that they would cease to continue as individual beings or cease to continue altogether. Peace in the tomb when this present toil is over seemed to them the most desirable of goods, and a dreamless sleep from which no angel trump should ever wake the sleeper.

"Two things," says Kant, "fill the soul with ever new and increasing admiration and reverence; the star-lit heavens above me, and the moral law within me."*

The Hebrews were the first to lend to the moral ideas a controlling influence in the sphere of religion. Let me attempt to briefly sketch the origin of Monotheism amongst them, as numerous considerations elsewhere recited in detail, have led me to conceive of it. The religions of the Semitic nations who surrounded ancient Israel were intensely emotional in

* Kant's Works (Rosenkranz edition) vol. viii. p. 312.

character, and their gods were gods of pleasure and pain. In the temples unbounded license alternated with self sacrificing asceticism. The lewd rites of the goddess of love must be regarded as typical of the one; the slaughter of sons in honor of Moloch, of the other. Now the Hebrews have been distinguished for the purity of their home life from a very early period of their history. The high value which they set on male offspring, the jealous vigilance with which they guarded the virtue of their women are alike illustrated in the narratives of the Bible. The more gifted and noble minded among them, beholding their domestic feelings outraged by the prevailing religions, rebelled against the gross conceptions of idolatry. How could they offer up their beloved sons for sacrifice, how could they give over their wives and daughters to shame? The controlling force of their character determined the doctrines of their creed. Judaism became, so to speak, a family religion. Jehovah is conceived of as the husband of the people. Israel shall be his true and loyal spouse, the children of Israel are His children. The image of Jehovah is that of the ideal patriarch. Like the patriarch, he is the head of the spiritual family of man. Like the patriarch in ancient times, he is the lawgiver and the judge; He is the guardian of domestic purity. The word for false religion in Hebrew signifies fornication. " Contend against your mother," says Jehovah, "for I am not her spouse, nor she my wife." "My people lust after false gods, for the spirit of impurity has seduced them." And the day of the triumph of the true religion is thus predicted: "On that day thou shalt not call me any more my Baal, (paramour) but thou shalt call me my husband, and I shall wed thee in justice, etc." Thus the idea of Jehovah sprang from the soil of the family, and the conception of a divine father in heaven was derived from the analogy of the noblest of moral institutions on earth. The spiritual God of the Hebrews was the personification of the moral Ideal.

Like his relations to the chosen people and to mankind in general, the relations of the Deity to the external world were described in accordance with the demands of the Ethical Law. Two things morality insists upon; first, that the natural in its coarser acceptation shall be subordinate to the moral. Secondly, that in the scale of values itself shall occupy the highest rank, and that the purpose of human life on earth can only be a moral purpose. As the mechanism of nature is not of itself calculated to harmonize with the purposes of spirit, it behooves that the spiritual God shall possess a power over matter adequate to enforce the claims of the moral ideal, such power as only the creator can exert over his creatures. Hence the doctrine of the creation. And again the state of perfection to which the human heart aspires can only be attained through the instrumentality of supreme wisdom, power and love, in a millennial age when the scheme of the universe will be perfected in the reign of absolute justice and peace. Hence the doctrine of the Messiah. Both doctrines are the typical expression of a moral need.

In the opening of Genesis we read a description of the making of the world. All was wild vast chaos, and darkness brooded over the abyss, when the Spirit of Jehovah breathed on the waters; a single word of command and light penetrated the gloom, the waters divided, the great luminaries started forth on their course; the earth clothed herself in verdure, and the forms of living beings sprang into existence. The words "God saw everything he had made and behold it was very good," contain the gist of the narrative. In Zephaniah and Isaiah we read: "On that day I will turn to the people a pure language that they may all call upon the name of the Lord to serve him with one consent." "No one shall then do evil, no one hurt in all my holy mountain, for the earth shall be full of the knowledge of God as the waters cover the sea."

These visions are not true in the sense of historical occurrences past or future. That the world was ever created out of nothing, what human understanding can conceive of it? That a time will come when society shall be so transformed that the pure language of love alone shall be spoken, who that is instructed in the failings of our finite nature can credit it? They are true in the sense of ideals; true, with the truth of poetry, bodying forth in concrete shape the universal yearnings of mankind.

There is also another element of belief associated with the doctrine of the Messiah, which still more plainly illustrates the typical value of religious tenets. In the coming week the churches throughout Christendom will rehearse the story of the passion and the death of their founder. Mournful chants and lamentations will recall every circumstance of the dark drama that closed on Calvary. That tale of harrowing agony still moves the hearts of millions as though it were a tale of yesterday. It is the symbol of the suffering and the crucifixion of the whole human race. "Ah, but our griefs he has borne, our sorrows he has carried, he was wounded for our transgressions, he was bruised for our iniquities." Hundreds of years before the birth of Christ, the author of these lines transcribed in them the sad experience of the reformers of his day. He does not refer to any one Messiah; he speaks of that legacy of sacrifice which is the heritage of the great and good, the world over. For who can help us when we are plunged in deepest anguish, when it seems as though we must sink under the load of trouble, but one who has endured like trials, endured and triumphed over them? It is the martyrdom of the pure that has redeemed mankind from guilt and sin? There is this constant atonement of the strong for the weak, of the good for the evil. As old Paul Gerhard has it in his seventeenth century hymn:

> " When utmost dread shall seize me,
> That human heart can know,
> Do thou from pain release me,
> By thy great pain and woe."

The teachings of religion then have their source in the aspirations of the human heart; are the echoes of our wishes and our hopes. Not valueless on that account, but valuable only in so far as they express in *noble* types, *noble* aspirations of our souls. It were sad indeed if morality depended upon the certainty of dogma. On the contrary it is true that all that is best and grandest in dogma, is due to the inspiration of the moral law in man. The time will come when the tenets of faith will no longer be narrowly understood as now; and while their influence will still be great, they will cease to be harmful and confining. They will be used as rare imagery, to deck the sublime meanings which they symbolize; not as vessels that contain the absolute truth, but as choice and beautiful vases, fit to hold the ever fresh and ever blooming flowers of the ideal.

The dogmatic assertion of religious teachings we hold to be a serious evil, and dogma as such we cannot accept. Its influence in the past has been pernicious, and is so at the present day no less. It has inflamed the hatred of man against his brother man, it has led to the fatal error of duties toward a personal Creator, distinct from our duties toward our fellows: it has perverted the moral sense, by giving to the concern of future salvation, a degree of prominence before which the interests of the present life sink into comparative insignificance; it does not afford us a common basis whereon we could unite, for it is by nature uncertain and calculated to provoke dissensions. On the other hand we behold in conscience the root of whatever good religion has achieved, and the law of conscience must suffice to guide and elevate our lives. To refresh the moral sentiment is the one thing needful in our time, and indeed presents a task on whose accomplishment the highest interests of society depend. Time will show that a simple appeal to duty will surely suffice to lead men to more earnest exertions toward the good. Time will show that those who know no other mode of salvation than the salvation which is attained by works of love, will be at least as active in the pursuit of virtue as those who put their trust in faith.

The gold of morality has been variously coined.

in the world's religious systems. Various have been the symbols that were stamped thereon, and various the images of the King in whose name it was issued, but their value so far as they had value was in the moral gold that they contained, and in naught else. Let Liberalism stamp its coin with the Eagle of Liberty only, in its ethical teachings it will still retain the substance of all religion.

Dogma we will keep in abeyance,—this is our point of departure, and the deed superior to the creed. Be it ours to hold high the moral ideal, whether we clothe it with personality or not. Be it ours to act divine things, no matter how we regard divine mysteries. Be it ours to help in lifting up the fallen, to lend free utterance to the complaints of the oppressed, to brand the social iniquities of our time, to give our hearts warmth and the labor of our hands to the cause of their redress, and to push on with whatever power we may, the progress of our race toward those high and holy goals of which the dreamers dream, the prophets prophesy.

III.

THE NEW IDEAL.

THE old religions and science are at war. With pitiless consistency science directs its attack upon their vulnerable positions. The conception of inexorable law subverts the testimony of miracles; the fond belief in truths divinely revealed fails to withstand the searching analysis of historical criticism; the battle of science is yet far from being won, but from our standpoint the issue cannot appear doubtful. It behooves us therefore to inquire into the moral bearings of the general result thus far achieved and to review what we have lost and won. Shall we succeed thereby in allaying the sense of alarm that is wont to agitate the timid heart when it beholds so much that it confidently believed a part of the everlasting verities of life, sink back into the gulf of uncertainty and doubt?

We are standing at the portals of a new age, and new conceptions have arisen of the purpose which we are here to accomplish and of the means of help we can command in the attempt to realize our destiny. These new conceptions we call The New

Ideal. It is the purpose of our present discourse to compare some salient features of the old and new.

The old and new Ideals agree in looking to an Infinite beyond the borders of experience, for it is in the nature of the ideal to lift us above the merely real. They differ in the direction in which they seek their object, and the bias which they consequently give to men's thoughts and actions. Theology, perceiving the inability of reason to solve the problems of the beginning and the end, yet unable to restrain a desire to know what is really unknowable, has impressed the imagination into its service, and drawn a picture of the transcendental world, conforming indeed to the analogies of man's terrestrial existence, but on this account all the more adapted to answer the wishes of the masses of mankind. Enough for them that they feel the need of believing the picture true. We of the New School are, if possible, even more profoundly convinced of the limitations of human reason. We cheerfully accord to the religious conceptions of the past a poetic value; they are poetry, often of the sublimest kind; but we cannot deceive ourselves as to the noble weakness of the heart to which they owe their origin; we cannot forget that in their case alas the wish has been father to the thought. To us the mystery is still mystery—the veiled arcana are not revealed, the riddle is unread. But we are not there-

THE NEW IDEAL.

fore filled with terror or dismay. In the moral nature of man we discover a divine element. In the voice of conscience we hear the voice of the present divinity within us, and we learn to regard this mortal state of ours as a channel through which the currents of Eternity ebb and flow ceaselessly. The divine nature is not far off, nor beyond the sea; in our own hearts on our own lips!

But let us seek to scrutinize the distinctive features of the old and new more closely. The old ideal was supernatural in character, it taught man to regard his life on earth as a brief, temporary transit, himself an exile from the Kingdom on high. The concerns of the present world were in consequence deemed of secondary importance, and the eye dwelt with anxious preference on the dim chances of the hereafter. Where the hope of immortality has been prominently put forward by any religion, the effect has thus but too often proved disastrous to the progress and security of society. It is well-known by what painful penances the monks of the Middle Ages sought release from the trammels of the flesh, how they affected to despise the ties of domestic affection, how they retarded the advancement of knowledge, how the passions which they sought in vain to suppress, often recoiled upon them with fearful retribution, and gave rise to disorders which seriously undermined public virtue.

But not only has supernaturalism tended indirectly to weaken the springs of virtue, it has called into being an order of men whose very existence is a standing menace to the freedom of intellect and the rights of conscience. The distance between the Creator and his creatures is so great, that the intervention of some third party is deemed necessary to mediate between the finite and the Infinite. The priest steps in to perform this office, and his influence is great in proportion to the value of the services which he is supposed to render. Furthermore it is believed that the personal deity requires the performance of certain actions in his honor, and what these actions are is again left to the priest to determine. In this manner the ceremonial part of religion grows up, and acquires a degree of importance fatal to the moral life. The duties toward God transcend the duties toward man, and but too often usurp their place.

The Bible likens the relations of man to God to those of a child to its father. It is true supernaturalism has often proved a valuable stay to those already morally strong, and it were absurd to deny that under its fostering care many of the noblest qualities that distinguish the filial relation have been developed in the lives of religious men. It is from no lack of appreciation on our part that we have dwelt on the evils rather than the blessings it has brought. But in acknowledging that we have really lost the sense of protection, the childlike trust which lend such rare beauty to the character of many ancient models of piety, we deemed it important to point to the shades that darken the picture of the supernatural religions, its lights are made the theme of a thousand discourses week after week, and are hardly in any danger of being speedily forgotten.

From the back-ground of the old Ideal stands out in bold relief the new. It is the reverse of supernatural; if it takes pride in anything, it is in marking a return to nature. Trammels of the flesh, contamination of the body? There is nothing it tells us in itself contaminating. The body is not alien to the mind, it is the seed plot from which mind flowers out in every part. Regard the form of man, observe the quick play of the features, the expressive smile, the speaking glance, every attitude, every gesture full of meaning, the whole body irradiated as it were, with the indwelling intelligence. And so the passions too which we are wont to associate with our corporeal nature are but the rough material from which the artist soul behind them fashions its immortal types of beauty and of holiness. There is a graceless inuendo in the term nature, as of something hard, gross, material. In truth, nature is the subtlest, most ethereal presence of which we catch a gleam only at rare intervals, the reflex of a hidden light that glimmers through the facts and motions of the world. Take the nature of water for instance. Is it in the hydrogen, in the oxygen, in the single atom? Not there, yet there! somewhere hovering, imponderous, elusive. It comes nighest to the senses when the atoms act and react upon each other, in the flow of mighty rivers, in the leap of cataracts, in the turmoil of the sea. Or the nature of the tree; is it in the roots, in the trunk, in the spreading branches, the leafy crown? Perhaps in the fruit more than elsewhere the hidden being of the tree comes forth into external reality, and opens to the eye and touch. In action and fruition the deeper nature appears. Thus in the outward world, and thus in man. Our soul-life, too, is a flowing stream, whose power is not in any part but in the ceaseless, changeful motion of the whole, that forms a strong spiritual current on which our thoughts and sentiments move like swimmers toward an infinite sea. And like a tree are we, with the mighty trunk of intellect, the spreading branches of imagination, the fibrous roots of the lower instincts, that bind us to the earth. But the moral life is the fruit we bear; in it our true nature is revealed; in it we see the purpose of our being fulfilled. So when we speak of a return to nature, it is this higher nature to which we refer, whose origin we know not, but whose workings we feel, and know them by the token of the sweet satisfaction they afford us to be the crown and glory of our lives. The old Ideal emphasizes the Eternal that is without us; the new the Eternal that is within ourselves. The old styles us exiles from the kingdom of truth; the new summons us to be the bannerbearers of truth; the old points to a heaven beyond the earth, the new tells us that our earth too is a part of the heaven, a light-world, among endless worlds of light.

If secondly we consider the means of support at our disposal in the pursuit of the ideal, we find prayer in universal use among the adherents of the old. Prayer in the sense of supplication, has been defined as " a request made to the Deity as if he were a man." And truly the language of prayer often tallies with this description. " Let me succeed in this undertaking," prays the Indian, "that I may slay my enemy and bring home the tokens of victory to my dear family, in order that they may rejoice together. Have pity on me and protect my life, and I will bring thee an offering." Some such inducement as the last is frequently coupled with the petition, "Here is an offering for you, O God! Look kindly towards this family, let it prosper and increase, and let us all be in good health." " Let me come upon my enemies speedily, let me find them sleeping and not awake, and let me slay a good many of them." " I pray for cattle, I pray for corn, I ask also for children, in order that this village may have a large population, and that your name may never come to an end, for of old we have lived by your favor, let us continue to receive it. Remember that the increase of our produce is the increase of your worship, and that its diminution must be the diminution of your rites." Among the Hindoos the efficacy ascribed to prayer was such that the gods themselves were deemed powerless to resist it, and the mystic invocations of the priests exerted a fateful influence on the destinies of the world. The ancient and modern literature of the Hebrews likewise testifies to their faith in prayer, and Christianity has herein followed if not outstripped their example. In case of drought the following prayer is offered in many of our churches: " Send us, we beseech thee, in this our necessity, such moderate rain and showers that we may receive the fruits of the earth to our comfort and to thy honor." In case of storms: "We humbly beseech thee to restrain these immoderate rains, wherewith for our sins thou hast afflicted us, and we pray thee to send such seasonable weather that the earth may in due time yield her increase for our benefit." In case of famine, " Increase the fruits of the earth by thy heavenly benediction, and grant that the scarcity and dearth which we now most justly suffer for our sins, through thy goodness may be turned into plenty." In case of sickness, prayers are offered for the recovery of the sufferer.

Against all these forms of petition the modern view of life emphatically protests. It starts with the grandest of scientific generalizations, that of the universality of nature's laws. These laws cannot be broken; they govern the course of the planets as they revolve through space, they appear in the slightest eddy of dust that rises on our streets. The world is a Kosmos; to pray for a change in its arrangements is to pray for its destruction. The rains come when they must come, and the earth yields or withholds her crop, as a system of causes determined from immeasurable æons of time prescribes. Is the God to whom men pray so poor a workman that he will change the mechanism of the Universe at their bidding? If all that is, is his work, why then the drought is his work, and the famine, and the sickness are his work, and they are, because he has willed that they should be. "The gods help them that help themselves." We are placed in a world with which we are but half acquainted; our business is to know it thoroughly. All the history of mankind from the beginning has been a series of tentative struggles to acquire this precious knowledge, and we have made indeed some headway. We began by defending ourselves against the attacks of wild beasts; we tilled the soil; we invented tools, we formed communities, we moderated the friction of social intercourse; we discovered the talisman of science, and the Aladdin's lamp of art. In the treatment of disease also a great advance has been made. When the Mayflower reached the American continent, she found a bleak and barren shore, full only of graves. A great epidemic had swept over the Indian tribes, and the natives fell like dead flies before the scourge. They had charms and prayers; these did not help them. We have accomplished a little; we are bound to aim at more. Why then call in the supernatural? It will not come, though we call never so loudly. The vain attempt does but keep us from that which is more needful, active exertion and strenuous efforts at self-help. But we are told that our success is poor at best, and that in the vast majority of cases, all our exertions avail nothing: moreover it is said that man is too frail and feeble a creature to depend upon himself alone in times of trial, and that prayer, whether it be answered or not, is valuable as a means of consolation that soothes and stills the heart. It is but too true that our achievements fall far short of our desires. Let those that do not, cannot pray, seek support in the sympathies of their kind, and where self-help fails, mutual help will offer them an inexhaustible source of strength and comfort. As for that species of prayer which is not addressed to a personal God at all, but claims to be an aspiration, an outpouring of the spirit, we do fail to see how it deserves the name of prayer in any sense. The use of the vocative, and of the pronoun thou is certainly calculated to mislead, and the appearance of inconsistency is hardly avoidable.

Lastly, the old Ideal was stationary, retrospective; it placed its paradise at the beginning of human history. In the far off past it beheld our best and loftiest hopes anticipated and realized. Then the full significance of life had been reached; then the oracles had spoken loudly and clearly whose faint echoes now float like memories of half forgotten melodies to our ear; then the imperishable truths were revealed in those olden, golden days. Not so, says the new Ideal. Rude and wretched were the beginnings of mankind on earth, poor the mind, and void the heart. Far from being exemplary, the ideas of right and wrong entertained by our earliest progenitors were infinitely below our own. Not indeed, that the substance of the moral sentiment has ever perceptibly changed. The inherent principle of right remains the same, but it assumes higher forms and is applied on a wider scale as the race advances. Thus the commandment not to kill a being like ourselves was recognized from the first, but in the earliest times, only members of the same family were esteemed beings like ourselves; to kill a neighbor was not wrong. The family widened into the clan, the clan into the people, and all the nations are now embraced in the common bond of humanity. Thus step by step the life of the clansman, the fellow citizen and at last of every human being came to be regarded as sacred. From a common centre morality has developed *outward in concentric circles*. In different ages also different virtues predominated. Patriotism was esteemed highest in the Roman world; self-sacrifice and chastity in the first Christian communities. But whatever had thus been gained was not thereafter lost. Each age added its own to the stock of virtue; each contributed its share to swell the treasure of mankind. The struggle for existence that raged fiercely on the lower levels of culture, loses its harsher aspects as we advance upon the path of civilization. The methods of force by which the unfit were eliminated are gradually falling into disrepute, if not into disuse. At last the good will survive because of its own persuasive excellency. The conflict will become one of ideas merely, an emulous peaceful contest for the prize of truth.

That the manners of the modern world have indeed become ameliorated, our own brief experience as a society serves to illustrate. A few centuries ago, such an enterprise as ours would never have been attempted, or if undertaken, would have been speedily crushed by the arm of authority or the weight of prejudice. We will not say that bigotry is dead; the fires of persecution still slumber beneath their ashes, and now and then start up into pretty bonfires to amuse the idle crowd; but the time has gone by when they could mount on funeral pyres—they can kindle conflagrations no more.

The new Ideal is progressive. Whatever we have achieved, it tells us there are larger achievements yet beyond. As we rise in the scale of moral worth, the eye becomes clearer and wider of vision. We see in remote ages a race of men freer and stronger because of our toils, and that is our dearest hope and our sweetest recompense that they shall reap what we have sown.

The old and the new Ideals will struggle for the mastery; that which is stronger will conquer as of old, in the struggle for existence. But the new hope fills us with trust and gladness that that which is true will be strong.

IV.

THE PRIESTS OF THE IDEAL.

It is with good reason, that the very name of the priesthood, has become odious to the modern mind. How has their fanaticism drenched the earth with blood, how has their unbridled ambition sown seeds of discord among the nations; how lamentable a commentary is the record of their frailties upon the assumption of superior sanctity and God-given authority. Yet it is not the priestly office, but its abuse, which has proved of evil, nor has the time yet come, when the ministry of priests can be safely dispensed with. There shall come a new Ideal to attract men's reverence and a new service of the Infinite and a new priesthood also to do its ministry. It is of this modern priesthood, I would speak.

Fear not that I am about to advocate a return to that system of spiritual bondage, from which we have but just escaped. The priests to whom we allude shall not be known by cassock or surplice. It is not at the altar they shall serve, least of all shall they have dogmas to communicate. They

THE PRIESTS OF THE IDEAL.

shall not be more than human, only if possible more human. Priests have we of science, we name them so; men whose whole soul is wrapped up in the pursuit of knowledge: priests of art, who dedicate their lives to the service of the Beautiful, priests also of the Moral, artists of the Good, sages in the science of Virtue, teachers of the Ideal.

Let us consider for a moment, in order to illustrate our meaning, the life of one such priest, whose fame has come down to us undimmed by the corroding influence of time—the life of Socrates. He held no office, he ministered at no shrine, yet he was in the true sense a priest. A plain unpretentious man, content to live on coarse fare, inured to want, homely in appearance, using homely language; nothing had he in appearance to attract; yet the gay youths left their feasts and frolics when he approached, and the busy market-place was hushed to listen to the strange wisdom of his sayings; there was indeed a singular and potent charm in this man s soul. He had a great need of righteousness, wonderful, how he awakened the same need in the hearts of the Athenian burghers of his day. He was the reverse of dogmatic. In comparison with the vastness of the unknown, he was wont to say, all human knowledge is little even to nothingness, he did not assume to know the truth, but strove to assist men in finding truths for themselves. He had his own enlightened views on questions of theology. But far from desiring to convert others to his convictions, he rather sought to divert their attention from those mysterious problems, in which men can never be wise, problems that are no nearer their solution to-day, than they were two thousand years ago. To those who questioned him concerning religion he replied: Are ye then masters of the humanities, that ye seek to pry into divine secrets? His father had been a fashioner of statues before him, he was a fashioner of souls! This Socrates was condemned to suffer death on the charge of atheism, and met his fate with the calmness of the philosophic mind. If death, he said, is progress to untried spheres, then welcome death! If it is sleep only, then also welcome death and its deep repose. All the tokens of the priest were fulfilled in him. He was true to himself and unbared to others the veiled truths of their own higher nature. He was a loftier presence on earth, a living flame fed from its own central being, a sun to which the world turned and was thereby enlightened. We perceive then, that what we desire is not a new thing. There has been this service of the Ideal from the earliest times. Only a new plea would we urge for larger fidelity to that which the best have striven for, and which under new conditions it will be the glory of our age to approach more nearly.

THE PRIESTS OF THE IDEAL.

The priest shall be a teacher of the "Ideal," but what is the Ideal and how distinguish it from the Real. Regard the trees, behold their number, the wondrous plenitude of their kinds. There is the lithe and slender pine, the mighty oak, the stately palm, the tender willow. Alike yet most unlike. And who has ever seen the perfect tree! Observe the expressive features of the human face. How many thousands of such faces are born into the world each year and yet no two alike. By what fine shades, what scarce perceptible curves, what delicate touches has nature's chisel marked them each apart. Graceful forms and lovely faces there are, yet perfect none. Now the Ideal is the perfection of the Real. To find it we must go beyond the Realities. We study the nature of the tree, of man. We note the suggestions of the various parts, complete and produce them in utmost harmony, each perfect in itself, each serving by its own perfection, the rounded symmetry of the whole. In the image thus created we grasp the ideal form. Art with its genial enchantments, creates such images and gives them permanence in pure types of immortal significance. Art is idealism of form.

The intellect also, which looks out from behind the features, the indwelling man, exhibits the same twofold aspect of the Real and Ideal. Our real thoughts are incomplete and inadequate. We are led astray a thousand times by false analogies, we are decoyed into the labyrinths of fancy, we become the victims of impression, the toys of circumstance. But deep down in the basic structure of the mind are true laws, unerring guides. Logic expresses them, logic is the idealism of intellect.

And lastly we recognize the same distinction in the realm of feeling. To the untutored caprice, the overmastering impulse, in brief to the realism of the passions is opposed the law of right feeling, which ethics expresses. Ethics is the idealism of character. We call this last the capital revelation of man's nature. The moral law is not derivative, it can not be proven, it can not be denied. It is the root from which springs every virtue, every grace, all wisdom and all achievement. An attempt has indeed been made to base morality upon a certain commonplace utility, but true morality scorns your sad utilities. That is useful, which serves an object besides itself, while morality is itself an end, and needs and admits no sanction save its own excellency. As it delights the man of science to expand his judgment in ever wider and wider generalizations, as the larger thought is ever the truer thought, so is there an exquisite pleasure and an unspeakable reward in expanding the narrow consciousness of self in the unselfish, and the larger emotion is ever the nobler emotion. We speak of the moral Ideal, as THE

IDEAL, because it expresses the central idea of human life, the purpose of our existence on earth. To expound and illustrate its bearings on our daily duties, our joys, our griefs and our aspirations, is the scope and limit of the priestly office.

The moral ideal would embrace the whole of life. Before it nothing is petty or indifferent, it touches the veriest trifles and turns them into shining gold. We are royal by virtue of it, and like the kings in the fairy tale, we may never lay aside our crowns. It tells us, that nothing shall be for its uses only, but all things shall take their tone and quality from the central idea.

When we build a house, it shall not be for its uses only. We shall have kitchens and drawing rooms and libraries and pictures and flowers, if possible. But the house, with all its comforts and luxuries, is mere framework, and our words and doings construct the true, the spiritual home. When we sit down to table, it shall not be for the use of the food and the flavor of the wine only, but morality should preside at the feast and lend it grace and dignity. Morality does not mope in corners, is not sour nor gloomy. It loves genial fellowship, loves to convert our meanest wants into golden occasions for joy and sympathy and happy communion. Manners too are the offspring of character. We do not rate highly the dry and cheerless conventionalisms of etiquette, but in their origin, they were the fruit of truth, and love. The rules of good breeding may be reduced to two; self-possession and deference. As when a public speaker loses his self-control, his own uncertainty is quickly communicated to his audience, and he forfeits his influence over his hearers; so the same cause produces the same effect in every lesser audience that gathers in our parlors. Society says to you: If I shall trust you, you must begin by trusting yourself. The man of the world will enter the palace of the prince and the cottage of the peasant with the same equipoise of manner. If he respects himself, there is no reason why he should stand abashed. Self-possession is essentially self-respect. Deference, too, is a primary condition of all courtesy. It teaches us to concede to others whatever we claim for ourselves; it leads us instinctively to avoid loudness, and self-complacency. It is expressed not only in the polished phrase, but in mien, attitude, every movement. Self-possession and deference of manner are both the outgrowth of moral qualities, the one depending on the consciousness of personal worth, the other inspired by an unselfish regard for the well-being of others. From these two it were possible to deduce the rules of a new 'Chesterfield,' which should be free from all the conceit and affectation of the old. Unfortunately, manners are no longer the natural outpouring of heart-goodness. Men attire themselves in politeness as they do in rich apparel; they may be as rude as they please, the year round, they know they can be fine on occasion. Moreover in the home circle, where the forms of courtesy are quite indispensable to prevent undue friction; to send the light of grace and poetry into a world of little cares; to fill the atmosphere of our daily surroundings as with the fragrance of a pervading perfume; they are yet most commonly neglected. The word manners has the same meaning as morals. When we shall have better morals, we shall have truer and sweeter manners.

The Ideal which thus seeks to interpenetrate the most ordinary affairs of private life, stands out also in the market place, in the forum, in the halls of legislation, and setting aside the merely useful, exhorts men to return to permanent values. That is the ideal view of politics which teaches us to hold the idea of country superior to the utilities of party, to exact worthiness of the public servants, to place the common good above sectional animosities and jealousies. That is the ideal view of commerce, which impels the merchant, while seeking prosperity by legitimate means, to put conscience into his wares and dealings and to keep ever in sight the larger purposes of human life. That is the ideal view of the professions, which leads their representatives to subordinate the claims of ambition and material gain to the enduring interests of science, justice, and of all the great trusts that are confided to their keeping. And he therefore shall be called a priest of the Ideal, who by precept and example will divert us from the absorbing pursuit of the realities and make plain to us that the real is transitory, while in the pursuit of the Ideal alone we can find lasting happiness. For the realities are constantly disconcerting us in our search for the better. They are so powerful, so insistent; we think them every thing until we have proved their attractions and find them nothing. We have that only which we are. But the common judgment holds to the reverse; we are only what we have. And so the turbulent crowd plunges madly into the race—for acres, for equipage, for well-stocked larders, for office, for fame. Good things are these, as scales on the ladder of life, but life is somewhat more than acres and equipage and office and fame. Seldom indeed do we truly live. Often are we but shadows of other lives. We affect the fashions not only in dress but also in thought and opinion. We are good or bad, as public opinion bids us. The state is ruined, the church is corrupted, and the world's giddy masquerade rushes heedlessly on.

Give me one who will think Having and Seeming less than Being; who will be content to be himself and a law unto himself and in him I will revere the ideal man. Before him the shams and mockeries of existence shall sink away. He will look into his own soul and tell you the oracles he has read there, and you will hear and behold your own heart. He will plant the sign of the Eternal on a high standard and call unto a people that strays in the wilderness to look up to that and be saved. The old and the young will he instruct, and they shall love him, for his words will be an articulate cry to the dumb voices in their own breasts. This is the be-all and end-all of his mission,—to make them acquainted with themselves. Do you know he will say, what a power is in you, what a light is hidden in the deep recesses of your nature. Artists are ye all to whom your own soul is given to mold it into beauty. Happy, happy indeed if you seek no other reward but the artist's joy in his work and know that to be your glory and your recompense.

It is well, that there should be priests appointed to bear such messages to us from time to time as we rest from our toil; to bring us face to face with the inner life. But there are special occasions in these passing years of ours, when the ideal bearings of life come home to us with peculiar force and when we require the priest to be their proper interpreter.

Marriage is one of them. We often hear it said that marriage is a mere legal compact. The state, it is true, has a vital interest in protecting the purity of the conjugal relation and may prescribe certain forms to which its citizens are bound to conform. But has the meaning of the new bond been indeed fully expressed, when the magistrate in the court room has pronounced the young man and the maiden to be now husband and wife? Among the ancient Hebrews youths and young girls were wont to meet on the Day of Atonement, the most solemn day of the year, the day of purification from sin, to cement their affections and plight their troth. For marriage itself was esteemed an act of purification. Marriage is the foundation of all morality. Its celebration does not end with the wedding day: it is a constant celebration, a perpetual intermarrying of two souls while life lasts.

Not the state only, but humanity also, that ideal state of which we are all citizens, has an interest in the contract. A new sanctuary is to be reared sacred to the ineffable mysteries of the home-life; in the home with all the tender and holy associations that cluster about it let it be dedicated. The supreme festival of humanity is marriage. There shall be music and joy and a white-robed bride with myrtle wreath; and solemn words to express the solemn meanings of the act.

THE PRIESTS OF THE IDEAL.

At the grave also is the office of the priest. When some dear friend has been taken from us, when the whole earth seems empty for the loss of one and the pillars of existence seem broken, he shall say to the grieving heart: Arise, be strong. He shall bid your brooding sorrow pause. He shall speak of larger duties, which they you mourn have left you, as their legacy. Larger duties: this is his medicine. You are not free, you poor and sadly stricken friends to stand aside in idle woe, but you shall make for the departed a memorial in your lives and assume their half completed tasks. So the loss, though loss it be, will purify you, and vim and vigor be found in the consolations of the Ideal.

We trust that we have used the term priest in no narrow restricted sense. It is not the hierarchies of the past or the present of whom we have spoken. The priest is not superior to his fellow men, nor has he access to those transcendental regions which are closed to others. His power is in this, that he speaks what all feel. And he shall be counted an acceptable teacher, then only, when the slumbering echoes within you waken to the music that moves and masters him.

There have been those, whose lives were molded on such a pattern among the clergy at all times, and it is this circumstance, that has attracted the reverence of mankind to the priestly office.

Noble men were they whose love burst through the cramping fetters of their creeds, apostles of liberty, missionaries of humanity.

But there is one other trait necessary to complete the picture. The priest of the Ideal must have the gift of tongues and kingly words to utter kingly thoughts. In the philosophy of Alexandria it was held, that before the world was, the word was, and the word created a universe out of chaos and the word was divine. With that heaven-born energy must he be filled, and with a breath of that creative speech must he inspire. No tawdry eloquence be his, no glittering gift of phrase or fantasy, but words of the soul's own language, words of the pith and core of truth.

The image of the Ideal priest which I have attempted to draw is itself an ideal image, nowhere realized, never to be fully attained. But it is to it that the priests of the new age will strive to come near and nearer, and that will be their pride and their happiness, if they can become in this sense friends and helpers of their kind.

In the eyes of the dogmatist they are strangers out of a strange land of thought. If you ask them for their pass word, it is freedom, if you ask for their creed, it is boundless. The multitude seeking to compress the infinite within the narrow limits of the senses, must needs have tangible shapes to lay hands on, names if nothing better. But the Ideal in the highest is void of form and its name unutterable. We will ascend on the wings of the morning, we will let ourselves down to the uttermost depths of the sea, and know it there. But chiefly within ourselves shall we seek it, in ourselves is its shrine. The time will come when single men shall no more be needed to do its ministry, when in the brotherhood and sisterhood of mankind all shall be priests and priestesses one to another, for all their life shall be a song of praise to the highest, and their whole being shall be consecrated and glorified in the immortal service of deathless Ideals.

V.

THE FORM OF THE NEW IDEAL.

A NEW ORDER.

I AM aware that there exists a deep seated prejudice in the minds of many of my hearers against what are called the forms of religion. We have too long experienced their limitations and restraints, not to be jealous now of our hard won liberties. But let us ask ourselves what it is that alienates our sympathies from the ritual and ceremonial observances of the dominant creeds? Is it the forms as such? Is it not rather the fact that to us they have become dead forms: that they no longer appeal to our sentiments, that they fail to stir, to invigorate, to ennoble us? We have not cast them aside lightly. Often have we entered the house of worship, prepared to be drawn back into the influence of its once familiar surroundings: we beheld again the great assembly, we heard the solemn music, we listened to the preacher as he strove to impress upon a silent multitude, the lessons of the higher life. But in the prayers we could not join, and the words to which the music moved we could not sing, and the maxims of the preacher were couched in language, and enforced with doctrinal arguments that touched no chord in our hearts. We left disappointed, we had received no help: if this were religion, we felt ourselves more distant from religion than ever before.

On the banks of the Euphrates there flourished of old an extensive colony of Jews. A "Prince of the Captivity" revived the memory of the vanished glory of King David's house. High schools were erected that afforded a common centre to the scattered members of the Jewish Faith. In these the people beheld at once their bond of connection with the past, and the pledge of future restoration to their patrimony. In the early part of the middle ages, a prayer for the health and prosperity of the presidents of the high schools was inserted into the liturgy. Well nigh eight hundred years have elasped since these dignitaries, and the schools themselves, have ceased to exist, yet the prayer is still retained, and may be heard repeated on any Sabbath in the synagogues of the orthodox—a prayer for the health of the Prince and the high schools on the Euphrates that vanished from the face of the earth eight hundred years ago. Thus do religious forms continue to maintain themselves long after their vitality is perished and their very meaning is forgotten. But if the prevalent forms have ceased to satisfy us, can we therefore dispense with form altogether? If the house that has given us shelter is in ruins, shall we therefore live in the woods and fields, or shall we not rather erect a new mansion on a broader foundation, and with firmer walls? It has been the bane of liberalism, that it was simply critical and not constructive. Your thought must have not wings only, but hands and feet to walk and work, to form and reform. Liberalism must have its organs, must enter the race with its rivals; must not criticise only, but do better. Liberalism must pass the stage of individualism, must become the soul of great combinations. What then shall be the form adequate to express the new Ideal?

The form of any religion is the image of its ideal. To illustrate what this means, let us consider for a moment the origin of the synagogue and the church.

The orthodox opinion that Judaism was revealed to Moses fourteen hundred years B. C. is condemned by modern critics of the Bible. The following are some of the considerations that have influenced their verdict. First, we read in scripture that so late as the reign of David, idolatry was still rampant among the Hebrews, and the attempt to explain this fact upon the theory of a relapse, is contrary to the testimony of the Bible itself.

Secondly: The name of Moses is unknown to

the prophets, his ostensible successors, a circumstance which would remain inexplicable if Moses had indeed been the founder of monotheism.

Thirdly: Large portions of the Pentateuch were probably not composed before the sixth or fifth century B. C., that is to say about a thousand years after the time of Moses. The account they give of the early history of the people is therefore open to serious and just doubt. The prophets were the real authors of monotheism. The priestly code of the Pentateuch does not represent the form of Judaism which they taught. They are not chargeable with the technicalities and dry formalism of the "Books of Moses." They were the avowed enemies of the priesthood and for a long time engaged in fierce struggles with the ruling hierarchy. Their doctrines were in the essence these: That there is a Creator, that he is just and merciful, that the same qualities in man are the most acceptable species of divine service, that God directs all events, whether great or small; and that it is the duty of man to accept the guidance of the Deity, and to follow with tireless diligence the clews of the Divine Will. Jehovah is to be reverenced not only as a spiritual, but also as a temporal sovereign, and the prophets are his ministers commissioned to transmit his decrees to men. Thus Monotheism found expression in the form of Theocratic government. It is true the heathen world was not yet prepared to enter into so near a relationship with the Creator. On this account the Jews were selected to be a typical people, and the Kingdom of God was for the time being confined to them. It is evident from the above that the order of the prophets was the very mainstay of the Theocratic fabric. When these inspired messengers ceased to appear, the conclusion was drawn that the Will of God had been fully revealed. The writings of the prophets were then collected into sacred books, and were regarded as the constitution of the divine empire. When Jerusalem was destroyed, the sacrifices were discontinued and Judaism was purged of many heathenish elements which had been allowed to mar the simplicity of the prophetic religion. The synagogue took the place of the Temple, and an intricate code of ceremonies was gradually elaborated, intended to remind the pious Jew at all hours and seasons of his duties toward God, and the peculiar mission accorded to his people. The synagogue was a single prominent peak in the range of the religious life, a rallying point for the members of the Jewish community, a meeting house where they assembled to confirm their allegiance to their heavenly King.

Now the cardinal point of difference between primitive Christianity and Judaism related to the alleged abrogation of the ancient constitution set forth in the old Testament. Christianity said: The

Messiah has come; the law of Moses is fulfilled; the King has issued a new constitution, and sent his own Son to put it in force. The time has arrived when the Kingdom of God need no longer be restricted to a single people. Jesus who perished on the cross will presently return, and the universal theocracy will then be proclaimed. But Jesus did not return, his followers waited long and patiently, but they waited in vain. As time rolled on, they learned to dwell less upon the expected Millennium on earth, and to defer the fulfilment of their hopes to the life beyond the grave. In the interval they perfected the organization of the church. The Christian Ideal of the Kingdom of Heaven is that of a communion of all saints under the sovereignty of God through Christ. The Christian Church is designed to be an image of this Ideal, a communion of saintly men on earth, accepting Christ as their Master. Christianity aspired to be the universal religion; there should be no barriers any more between man and man; the exclusiveness of ancient Judaism should be broken down; yet withal the barriers of a new creed soon arose in place of the old; the portals of the Kingdom of Heaven were rigidly closed against all who refused to bow to the despotism of dogma; and the virtues of pagans were declared to be shining vices. The moral teachings of Christ are gentle and kindly, but in the doctrinal contentions of the Christians the spirit of the Master was forgotten, and the earth was deluged with blood.

And now the new Ideal differs from Christianity in this, that it seeks to approach the goal of a Kingdom of Heaven upon earth, not by the miraculous interference of the Deity, but by the laborious exertions of men, and the slow but certain progress of successive generations. We have named the form of religion an image of the Ideal, yet an image poor and incomplete at best, rather a symbol, a suggestion of what can never be realized. In the realm of art we do not find the soul of beauty in the colored canvas or the marble statue; these are helpful hieroglyphics only, teaching those that can read their mute language to create anew the ideal as it lived in the artist's soul, in the divine hour of conception. Thus all form has its value only in what it suggests. Our Ideal is that of the fellowship of humanity in highest wisdom, highest truth and highest love. The form of this ideal therefore can be none other than a new fellowship united by the higher truths and purer love that make its bond to be a symbol of the highest! We are weary of the unreal and untrue existence we are forced to lead; we are weary of the emptiness of routine, weary of the false coin of reputation that passes current in the market of vanity fair; we are weary of the low standards by which actions are judged, and to which, to our dismay, we perceive our actions insensibly conform. But the pressure of social influences about us is enormous, and no single arm can resist it. We must needs band together then, if we would achieve a higher life ; we must create for ourselves a purer atmosphere, if any rarer virtues are to flourish in our midst ; we must make our own public opinion, to buoy us up in every loftier aspiration. Unions we want that will hold, not religion as a duty, but duty as a religion ; union to achieve a larger morality. Three things morality demands of us as interpreted in the light of our present social conditions: greater simplicity in manners, greater purity in the passions, greater charity.

The habit of luxurious living is eating into the vitals of society, is defiling the family, and corrupting the state. Let me not be falsely understood. All that is luxury which political economists are wont to class as unproductive consumption. In this sense, books, music and pictures are luxuries, and who would be willing to forego them. It becomes us to the utmost of our powers to satisfy the thirst for knowledge, and to educate the sense of harmony: it is wise to expend generously upon every means of culture and refinement. But this we must bear in mind, that there should be a rank and a proper subordination among our tastes and desires. Now that is luxury in the evil, in the debasing sense of the term, that we subvert the natural order of our tastes, that we make the mere gratification of the animal passions, the mere pursuit of wealth, the mere adornment of our clay, main objects, while the graces of intellect perish, and the adornment of the soul is neglected. Say not, we will do the one, and not leave undone the other; for the inordinate degree to which the meaner passions are developed, dulls our sense of loftier needs. We cannot serve these two masters. Frivolous in prosperity, we become helpless in adversity and perish inwardly, our growth stunted, our nobler sympathies blunted, long before we are bedded in our graves. What single effort can achieve a change? Fellowship, friends are needed, and a public opinion on behalf of simplicity.

And purity in the passions is needed. An ugly sore is here concealed, a skeleton in the closet of which men speak with bated breath. Is there not such a thing as sanctity of the person! Did you not rebel against human slavery because you said it was wrong that any being born in the image of man should be the tool of another? And no arguments could deceive you—not if the slave offered himself willingly to the yoke, and rejoiced in his bondage. You dared not so sin against human nature, and accept that offer. And yet New York has its slaves, Boston its slaves, and every large town on the face of the wide earth has this sinful, outcast army of slaves—tools, whom we have robbed of that which no human being has a right to barter, the right to virtue at least, if not to happiness. Call not that a law of nature, which is the lawlessness of nature! Say not, it has ever been thus, and ever shall be! From depths of vice which the imagination dare not recall, humanity has slowly risen to its present level, and higher and higher will it take its course when the conscience is quickened and true love expands. Fellowship is needed to support this difficult virtue and a public opinion on behalf of purity.

And charity, friends; not that which we commonly called charity; but charity that prevents rather than cures. You pass through the lower quarters of our city, you see the misery, the filth, the gaunt, grim poverty, the careworn faces, the candidates for starvation. Starvation! whoever hears of it? The newspapers rarely speak of it; here or there an exceptional case. Nay truly, these people do not starve; they die of a cold perhaps; the small-pox came and carried them off: diphtheria makes its ravage among them. Ah, but was it not want that sapped their strength, and made them powerless to resist disease? Was it not their life of pinched pauperism that ripened them for the reaper's scythe? Then pass from these sorrowful sights to our stately Avenue. Behold the gay world of fashion, its painted pomp, its gilded sinfulness, its heartless extravagance. Is not this an intolerable contrast? Shall we rest quiet under the talk of irremediable evils? Is it not true that something must be done, and can be done because it must? The distribution of wealth they say, is governed by economic laws, and sentiment has no right to be considered in affairs of business. But where I pray you is the sentiment of brotherly love considered as it should be? Educate the masses! But do we educate them? Stimulate their self-respect and teach them self-help! But what large or effective measures are we taking to this most desirable end? You cannot help, good friend, nor I. But a dozen might aid somewhat, and a thousand brave unselfish hearts knit together for such a purpose, who shall say what mighty changes they could work. Surely fellowship is needed here, and a public opinion on behalf of charity.

The "fine phrase," humanity has pregnant meanings. They stand for the grandest, the sternest realities of the times. Purity, charity and simplicity, these shall be the watchwords of a new fellowship, which shall practice the teachings of humanity, that are vain as the empty wind, if heard only and approved, but not made actual in our deeds.

And yet some will smile incredulously and ask,

Where are the men and women prepared to undertake such a task? It is true, we must begin at the beginning. From earliest childhood the young must be trained on a nobler method, and in the ethical school lies the main work of preparation. There every step in the course of development must be carefully considered, vigilantly watched and wisely directed, to the one crowning purpose of ripening the young minds and hearts for that fellowship of love and hope.

A new fellowship, a new order, I say boldly, whose members shall not be bound by any vows, which shall have no convents, no mysteries, but shall make itself an exemplar of the virtues it preaches, a form of the ideal. The perils that attend such organizations are great; we will not attempt to underrate their gravity, but we believe they can be overcome. The spirit of co-operation lends mighty momentum to every cause; it depends upon the cause itself whether the influence exerted shall be for good or evil. And there has been in history a single order at least of the kind which I describe: "The brotherhood of the common life," it was called; an order composed of earnest, studious men, to whom the upheaval of Europe in the sixteenth century was largely due; a noble brotherhood that prepared the way for the great Reformation. The Catholic orders are dedicated to the world to come;

the order of the Ideal will be dedicated to the world of the living: to deepen and broaden the conscience of men will be its mission.

The propaganda of Liberalism in the past has been weak and barren of great results. Strong personalities it has brought forth; around these societies have clustered and fallen asunder when the personal magnet was withdrawn. What we need is institutions of which persons shall be merely the exponents; institutions that must be grounded on the needs of the present, and that shall last by their own vitality, to future ages and to the increase of future good.

It is the opening of the spring.* After its long winter sleep, the earth reawakens, and amid the fierce storms of the Equinox nature ushers in the season of flowers and of summer's golden plenty. It is the day of Easter. Loudly the bells are pealing and joyous songs celebrate in the legend of "Christ risen from the grave," the marvel of the Resurrection. What we cannot credit of an individual, is true of the nations. After long periods of seeming torpor and death, humanity ever arises anew from the dust, shakes off its slumbers, and clothes itself with fresher vigor and diviner powers.

Let the hope of the season animate us. Let it

---

* The above discourse was delivered on Easter Sunday, April 1st, 1877.

fill our souls with confidence in our greater destinies; let it teach us to trust in them and to labor for them, that a new Ideal may vivify the palsied hearts and a new spring tide come, and a new Easter dawn arise over all mankind.

VI.

THE RELIGIOUS CONSERVATISM OF WOMEN.

No thoughtful person can fail to appreciate the enormous influence which women are constantly exercising for good and evil upon the destinies of the world. The charms and graces of existence, whatever ennobles and embellishes life, we owe mainly to them. They are the natural guardians of morality, and from age to age the mothers of households have preserved the sacred fire on the domestic hearth, whereat every virtue is kindled. But they have also been the most formidable enemies of progress. Their conservatism is usually of the most unreasoning kind, and the tenacity with which they cling to favorite prejudices is rarely overcome either by argument or appeal. They have been from time immemorial the dupes, the tools, and the most effective allies of priestcraft. Their hostility to the cause of Reform has been so fatal, not only because of the direct influence of their actions, but because of that subtle power which they exert so skilfully over the minds of husbands, brothers and friends, by the arts of remonstrance, entreaty and the contagion of their feeble alarms. The question whether their hostility can be turned into friendship, is one of momentous importance for the leaders of the Liberal movement to consider.

In the following we shall endeavor to make plain that the subordinate position hitherto assigned to women, is the principal cause that has impelled them to take sides against religious progress.

Among the primitive races woman was reduced to a condition of abject slavery. Affection of the deeper kind was unknown. The wife was robbed or purchased from her relations; was treated as a menial by her husband, and often exposed to the most brutal abuse. As civilization advanced, the marriage bond became more firm, and common interest in the offspring of the union served to create common sympathies. Among the Greeks, the ideal of domestic life was pure and elevated. The tales of Andromache, Penelope and Alcestes illlustrate the strength of conjugal fidelity and the touching pathos of love that outlasts death. The Grecian home was fenced about with scrupulous care and strictest privacy protected its inmates from temptation. It was the duty of the wife to superintend the internal economy of the household, to spin and weave, to direct the slaves in their various occupations, to nurse them when sick, to watch over the young children, and chiefly to insure the comfort and satisfaction of her lord. His cares and ambitions indeed she hardly shared. She never aspired to be his equal, and simple obedience to his wishes was the supreme virtue impressed upon her by education, and enforced by habit. Among the Romans, the character of the matron is described in the most laudatory and reverential terms. Still the laws of the Republic made woman practically the bondswoman of man. It is well-known that our English word family is derived from the Latin where it originally means the household of slaves. The matron too, was counted, at least theoretically, among these slaves, and the right of deciding her fate literally for life or death, belonged exclusively to her husband. It is true in the cordial intimacy of the monogamic bond, the austerity of usage, and the harshness of the laws are often tempered by affection and mutual respect; yet we are aptly reminded by a modern writer on this subject, that the law which remains a dead letter to the refined and cultivated becomes the instrument of the most heartless oppression in the hands of the vulgar and the passionate.

Among the Hebrews, a position of great dignity and consequence was sometimes accorded to their women. The wives of Abraham, Isaac and Jacob played an important part in directing the affairs of the Patriarchal households. A woman performed the functions of judge and leader of armies, women sat upon the throne, prophetesses were consulted in grave matters of the State and of religion; in the absence of sons, the Mosaic law guarantees to daughters the right of succession to the family estate. The later writings of the Jews are likewise replete with noble sentiments touching the sanctity of the conjugal tie. Many of the ordinances of the Talmud depend upon women for their execution, and this circumstance alone must have contributed to raise them in the popular estimation. In every marriage contract a certain sum was set apart for the wife, in case of her husband's death or of divorce. Still the right of dissolving the matrimonial connection belonged exclusively to the husband, although under certain conditions he could be forced by the court to issue the "writ of separation." However the wife might be honored and loved, she was ever regarded as man's inferior.

The influence of Christianity upon the position of women, was twofold, and in opposite directions. On the one hand women had been among the first and most devoted followers of Jesus; women were largely instrumental in effecting the conversion of the Roman Empire, and in the list of martyrs, their names shine preëminent. On the other hand, the church in the early centuries cast an unpardonable slur on the marriage relation. We read of young maidens fleeing the society of dear companions and friends, to escape the temptation of the affections, of faithful wives, filled with inexpressible loathing at a connection which they deemed contrary to the dictates of religion, and deserting husbands and children. The desire of love was poisoned with a sense of guilt. The celibacy of the clergy, finally enforced by Pope Hildebrand, gave rise to the most shocking irregularities. All this tended to degrade the female sex.

At the time of the crusades a partial revulsion of feeling took place. The spirit of chivalry entered the church, the character of woman was transfigured, and the worship of the Virgin Mary spread in consequence throughout Europe. A change in the education of girls was one of the results of the rise of Chivalry. Music and poetry became its chief elements; women were fed on intellectual sweetmeats, but strong and healthy nourishment was still denied them.

In all the different stages of progress which we have thus rapidly scanned, the assumption of man's superiority to woman was held as an incontestible article of belief, and even the chivalric ideal is only a more amiable and disguised expression of the same view.

What effect the disabilities under which they

labored must have had upon the religious life of women will readily be perceived. There are two attitudes of mind peculiarly favorable to orthodoxy; the one a tendency to lean on authority, the other a disposition to give free sway to the feelings without submitting them to the checks of reason. Now it is plain that the condition of dependence to which society has condemned woman is calculated to develop these very qualities to an abnormal degree. From early childhood she receives commands and is taught to distrust her own judgment. When she enters the bonds of matrimony she becomes dependent on her husband for support, and in the vast majority of cases, his riper judgment shames her inexperience. In all graver matters she must perforce defer to his decision. Accustomed to rely on authority, is it surprising that in matters of religion, where even men confess their ignorance, she should rejoice in the authority of the priest, whose directions relieve her of doubt and supply a ready channel for her thoughts and acts. Again the feelings are her natural weapons, shall she not trust them! The stability and security of society are the conditions on which her dearest hopes depend for their realization. Can she welcome the struggles of innovation. All her feelings cluster about the religious traditions of the past; all a woman's heart pleads for their maintenance.

Now to confine the feelings of woman within their proper bounds, it is necessary to give wider scope, and a more generous cultivation to her intellect; in brief to allow her the same freedom of development as is universally accorded to man. Freedom makes strong, and the confidence of others generates an independent and self-reliant spirit in ourselves. It is indeed often urged that woman is by nature the inferior of man. But the appeal to physiology seems to be at least premature; the relation of the size of the brain to intellectual capacity being by no means clearly determined; while the appeal to history is, if possible, even more treacherous, because it cites the evils engendered by an ancient and long continued system of oppression in favor of the system itself. Counting all the disadvantages against which woman has been forced to contend, and which have hampered her every effort to elevate her condition, it is truly marvelous, not that she has done so little, but that she has accomplished that which she has. Even in the difficult art of government she has earned well merited distinction, and women are named among the wisest and most beneficent rulers of ancient and modern times.* What the possibilities of woman's nature may be, no one can tell; least of all she herself. As it is she is credited with a superior power of

* J. S. Mill, The Subjection of Women, p. 100.

intuition, a readier insight into character, a more complete mastery of details. What larger powers now latent a broader culture will bring to light, remains for the future to show.

But we are told that the sphere of woman's work is in the home, and that properly to perform her vocation there, she does not need the vigorous training required for men. That woman's mission ought to be and happily is in the majority of cases in the home, no one will gainsay. At the same time, we should not close our eyes to patent facts, facts such as these ; that the number of women whose mission actually does not lie in the home, is exceedingly great ; that according to the last census of the United States, for instance, the female population of the State of New York, is fifty-six thousand in excess of the male ; that well nigh two millions of women in this country are engaged in working for their livelihood. Is it not cruel mockery to say to these women that their business is in the household? If the condition of things is such that they must seek outside labor; if we permit them to toil by hundreds of thousands in the fields and factories, on what plea of right or reason can we deny them admission to the higher grades of service ? Is it not simple justice to admit them to all the professions, and to allow them the same advantages in colleges and professional schools as are enjoyed by men?

We need not fear that the privilege will be abused If women undertake to engage in pursuits for which they are physically or mentally unfit, the effect of competition will quickly discourage them, and here as elsewhere, only the fittest will survive.

But aside from those who are destined to remain single, and considering the seven millions of women, or more, who will become wives and mothers of families; is not the demand for higher education equally imperative in their case? Young girls are but too often educated to be the agreeable companions, rather than the partners of their future husbands. They receive sufficient instruction to give them a general acquaintance with the surface of things, but not sufficient to develop what ought to be the chief end of every scheme of education—*a permanent intellectual interest in any one direction.* Much time is wasted on minor accomplishments. At an age when the young girl is still totally immature, she is often withdrawn from the influence of her preceptors, and hurried from dissipation to dissipation, to tread the round of society's gayeties, and to inhale the poisonous atmosphere of flattery and conventional falsehoods. She enters a new world. The contrast between the restraints of school life, and her novel sense of consequence intoxicates her; the desire for pleasure becomes a passion; the books of useful information, that never possessed a real charm for her, are cast aside, and the literature of the sentiments alone retains its attractions during the remainder of life. It is not astonishing that those whose minds are thus left barren, should employ their leisure hours in frivolous or vicious occupations; that an exorbitant luxury, the sign at all times, of deficient culture, should have infected the community. It is not wonderful that when the trials of life approach, these women grasp wildly at the nearest superstition, and prostrate themselves before any idol of the vulgar, in their blind ignorance and credulity.

I have said that higher education can alone make marriage what it ought to be, for it is not fancy or the glow of passion that can bind the hearts together in lasting wedlock. The marriage bond has deeper meanings. Two souls are united, each to be all in all to each. Here shall be the very consummation of love; love, that precious boon that assuages every pang, and stills every grief, and triumphs over sickness, sorrow, and the tomb. All nature's symbols fail to express its fulness; it has the hope of the dawning day; it has the tender pathos of the light of the moon; it has the melody of birds, the mystic stillness of the forest, the infinity of the fathomless sea! Bounteous love, how inexhaustible are its treasures! The fires of the passions kindle affection, but cannot secure it. If there be only the stubble of desire in the heart, that will quickly be consumed; if there be veins of true gold there, that will be melted and refined. Years pass, youth fades, the attendant train of the graces vanishes, loveliness falls like a mask, but the union only becomes firmer and trustier, because it is a union, not of the sentiments merely, but of the souls. The wife becomes the true sharer of her husband's thoughts; mutual confidence reigns between them; they grow by mutual furtherance; each sees in each the mirror of his nobler self; they are the true complement one to the other. Who does not know that such unions are rare! Common sympathies, common duties do indeed create a tolerable understanding in most households; but that is not wedlock that men and women should jog on tolerably well together for the better part of a lifetime.

The modern mind is constantly broadening; new facts, new discoveries are constantly coming to light, and loftier problems engage the attention of thinkers. If woman would not be utterly left behind in the race, then must she make an effort to acquire more solid knowledge, and educational reform is the first step in the cause of woman's emancipation. The electoral franchise, and whatever other measures may be included in the popular phrase of "Woman's rights" should be reserved for future discussion. If practicable at all, they are assuredly for the present of secondary importance.

Permit me to close by briefly formulating a few points that seem to me to deserve special consideration in this connection.

Woman, like man, should comprehend the age in which she lives and the great questions by which it is agitated. To this end a knowledge of history, and chiefly the history of her own nation, is requisite. She should learn to understand the principles of the language she speaks, and the literature in which it is preserved, not from dry text-books, but from the living works of the authors themselves. She should be able to pass an intelligent judgment upon the political issues of the day, that take up so large a share of men's conversation, and to this end the rudiments of political science might profitably be taught her. She should possess sufficient familiarity with the natural sciences to comprehend at least the main results of scientific investigations, and a training of this kind would have the further advantage of accustoming her mind to the methods of accurate thinking. She should gain some knowledge of the human body and of the laws upon which its health depends. Is it not strange that this important branch of knowledge is so generally neglected in the training of those who are to be mothers of the future generation? How often would proper attention to a few simple rules of hygiene prevent sickness; how often would more efficient nursing avert death, where it is now freely allowed to enter. Then too the outlines of pedagogy should be included in a course of advanced instruction for women. Mothers are the educators of the children, but the educators themselves require to be educated.

If the intellect of girls were braced and stimulated in this manner, they would exhibit greater self-possession and self-reliance in their later lives; they would be less apt to be deluded by false appeals to the feelings: "the woman's view" would be no longer proverbial for the weaker view; the whole of society would feel the beneficent change, and the problem which we set out to discuss in the beginning would in due time solve itself.

We do not for a moment apprehend that the increased cultivation of the intellect would entail any loss of sweetness or of those gracious qualities that make the charm of womanhood. Wherever such a result has been apparently observed, it is safe to ascribe it to other causes. Truth and beauty are far too closely akin in their inmost nature to exclude each other. Nor do we fear that the intensity of moral feeling, for which women are distinguished, would suffer under the restraining influence of reason's guidance. The moral feelings would indeed be purified, elevated and directed to their proper objects by the judicious use of reason; they would not therefore be enfeebled. In the past, the conservatism of women has been a mighty obstacle in the path of progress. It is but just to add that at the dawn of every great religious movement which promised the moral advancement of the race, gifted women, rising above the weakness of their sisters, have been among the earliest to welcome the new hope for humanity; have been among the most ardent, the most self-sacrificing of its disciples. The Liberal movement of our day also is essentially a movement for larger morality, and more and more as this feature will be clearly developed, may it hope to gain the sympathies of brave and good women to its side. In their support it will behold at once the criterion of its worthiness, and the surest pledge of its ultimate triumph.

VII.

OUR CONSOLATIONS.*

WE go out in these balmy days of spring into the reviving fields, and the eye drinks in with delight the fresh and succulent green of the meadows; the willows begin to put forth their verdant foliage, the brooks purl and babble of the new life that has waked in the forest: be glad, all nature cries, summer is coming. And the freshness of the season enters into our own hearts, our pulses beat more quickly, our step is more buoyant. We remember all that is joyful in existence; the arts that embellish, the aspirations that ennoble, the affections that endear it. Golden the future lies before us; our very cares lose their sombre hues; like the golden islands of cloud that glow in the glory of sunset skies.

But beneath the fair semblance of nature that for a time deludes our senses, a dark and terrible reality is concealed. Observe how pitilessly the destructive elements pursue their path, the earthquake the

* A discourse delivered on Sunday, April 29, 1877.

OUR CONSOLATIONS.　　　　119

tornado, the epidemic. A few months ago a rise of the sea swept away two hundred thousand human lives in the course of a few hours. Myriads of sentient beings are daily cast up in the summer to perish with the first breath of cold. In the animal world, the strong feed upon the weak, and the remorseless struggle for existence extends even into the sphere of human activity. At this very moment the whole of Europe is filled with anxious alarm in view of an impending war of conquest. While industry is paralyzed, while trade is at a stand-still, while a virulent disease generated by starvation has broken out in Silesia, and the workmen of Lyons have become dependent on the public charity of France, the resources of nations, already well nigh exhausted, are drained to prepare for the emergencies of conflict. With a secret thrill of terror we read that beds for the wounded and millions of roubles for hospital appliances are being voted by the municipalities of Russia. Readily the imagination can picture to itself what these ghastly preparations mean. It is true, so long as all is well with us, the larger evils of the world do not greatly disturb our equanimity. Man has the happy faculty of abstracting his attention from things remote. The accumulated woes of a continent affect us less than some trifling accident in our immediate vicinity. But when the messengers of evil have cast their shadows across our threshold, when calamity has laid its heavy hand upon our shoulder, it is then that the general unsatisfactoriness of life recurs to us with added force in view of our own experience; the splendor fades from the surrounding scene; every dark stain takes on a deeper blackness, and the gloom that comes from within fills and obscures the entire field of our vision. We have sustained financial loss, perhaps we are harrowed by domestic discord, we are suddenly stricken in the midst of health, and drag on long years as hopeless invalids, or worse still, we stand at the bedside of some dear friend or kinsman, see him stretched upon the rack of pain, and can do nothing to alleviate his sufferings; we see the end slowly nearing; but oh, the weary waiting, the patient's agonizing cry for death, the cruel struggle that must still intervene. And when at last, it is over, and we have laid him away under the sod, and returned to our desolate homes, what hope remains! Whither now, we ask, shall we turn for consolation? Is there no outlook from this night of trouble? Is there no winged thought, that will bear us upward from out the depths; is there no solace to assuage our pangs?

Among the means of consolation commonly recommended the doctrine of Immortality seems to be regarded as the most appropriate and effective. It is needless to lament; the deceased has entered a better life. Yet a little and you will join him to be no more parted. Nor can we deny that to those who cordially entertain it, the belief in the soul's immortal continuance becomes a source of pure and inexpressibly tender satisfaction. But with a certain class of minds—and their number, I believe, is on the increase—the consoling influence of this doctrine is marred by the fatal uncertainty in which the whole question is involved, and which no efforts of man have ever yet, nor ever will, avail to remove. Christianity indeed claims to have settled the point. The Deity himself, it avers, intervened by direct revelation from on high, to set our doubts at rest, and Jesus when he arose on the third day forever deprived the grave of its sting and took away our fears of the tomb. But to those who read the books of revelations with unbiased mind, the fact of their human authorship becomes sadly apparent, and the resurrection itself is as difficult to prove as the doctrine which it is designed to substantiate.

In modern times spiritualism has likewise endeavored to demonstrate to the senses the existence of a world of souls beyond our own. But the phenomena on which it lies are in part disputed, in part the interpretation put upon them, must, to say the least, be regarded as premature.

Moreover we should remember that even if by some unknown means the fact of immortality could be established, the question of our re-union with friends in the hereafter, in which alone the heart of the mourner is interested, would still remain an open one and might be answered in the negative. The belief in immortality has been held in this way by some of the greatest intellects of the human race, Spinoza among the rest. If we knew that we shall continue to live, we should not therefore know how we shall continue to live. Perhaps it might prove that all our previous connections would be severed; and who can tell what new phases of existence, what endless metamorphoses might await us among the infinite possibilities of Eternity.

So deep seated is the sense of uncertainty concerning our fate beyond the tomb, that no religion, however great the control which it exerted over men, has ever been able to banish it entirely from their hearts. The most ardent Christian is hardly less anxious than the infidel to retain those who are dear to him in life. He prays as fervently for their health as though their present state were the sum total of their existence. And yet he should rather hail the day of death as a day of thanksgiving, and rejoice that those whom he loves have been translated to a sphere every way so much more desirable than our own. No, the natural feeling cannot be suppressed, loss is felt to be loss, and death remains death. No hope of a happier condition in the world to come, no confidence in the promises and prophesies of faith, can efface the sense of present bereavement, and as we all alike feel it, so are we all, believers and unbelievers, interested in seeking the means of its present relief.

Some of the most fervid, religious natures of the past endeavored to escape the sorrows of the world by having recourse to the cruel remedy of asceticism. The ascetic ponders the origin of suffering: he sees that the desire for pleasure is the cause of pain. Were we not eager to possess we should not regret to lose. He cuts the gordian knot saying, abjure desire! When you cease to want, you shall no longer be bruised. There are certain wants inherent in the body—the want of food, drink, sleep; the heart has its needs—friendship, sympathy; the mind—knowledge, culture. All these should be subdued. We should eat and drink the coarsest in quality and the least possible in quantity; we should avoid the attachments of love; we should be poor in spirit, and despise wisdom. The ascetic ideal took firm root in Christianity at an early period of its history. The extravagance of the Egyptian anchorites is well known. The "pillar saint," St. Simeon, who is said to have passed some thirty years of his life on the summit of a column twenty yards in height, taking only the scantiest nourishment, eschewing ablutions, covered with filth and sores, was worshipped as a holy man by the multitude and his example was followed by others, though with less rigor, during a period of nearly a thousand years. Among the Hindoos, too, the ascetic ideal acquired a baneful ascendency. We can hardly credit the tales that have come to us concerning the insane fanaticism which raged amongst this people. To what tortures of body and soul did they subject themselves, what cruel ordeals did they invent in order to steel themselves against the inevitable sufferings of life. It was their beau-ideal to achieve a state bordering upon absolute unconsciousness, in which the power of sensation might be entirely blunted, and even the existence of the physical man be forgotten.

This, indeed, is a capital remedy, a species of heroic treatment that attains its end. Man becomes passive in pain, incapable of sorrow, unmoved by any loss. But with the pains, the joys of existence have likewise fled. The human being walks as a shadow among shadows, a soulless substance, the wretched semblance of his former self. Who would not rather bear the heaviest ills that flesh is heir to, than purchase his release at such a cost.

And now in setting forth our own view of this mighty problem of human sorrow, let us bear in mind that our private hardships and those general evils which we see enacted on a scale of such appalling magnitude in the world around us, must be considered together, for the same cause constantly gives rise to both. It is of the utmost importance that we should weigh well what we have a right to expect, and ponder the conditions on which humanity holds the tenure of its existence. Perhaps our deepest disappointments are often due to the fact that we ask more than we have any legitimate title to receive, and judge the scheme of the Universe according to false analogies and preconceived notions which the constitution of things does not bear out. We are subject to two laws, the one the law of nature, the other that of morality: the two clash and collide, and a conflict ensues. Theology labors to show that this conflict is apparent rather than real, to admit it would seem to impugn the justice of the Deity. Thus we read in the Old Testament that when the sufferer Job protested his innocence, his friends assailed his veracity, and persisted in holding the bare fact of his misfortune as unimpeachable evidence of his sinfulness. And thus the Psalmist assures us, that he has grown old and never seen the righteous man in want. The experience of the Psalmist must have been limited indeed! The conflict exists, however it may be denied. Nature is indifferent to morality, goes on regardless. The great laws that rule the

Kosmos, act upon this planet of ours, nor heed our presence. If we chance to stand in the way, they grind us to pieces with grim unconcern: the earth opens, the volcano sends forth its smoldering fires, populous cities are overwhelmed, locusts devastate the country; they do not pause before the field of the righteous; they have no moral preference. The seeds of disease also are scattered broadcast over the land, and the best, often those whom we can least afford to lose, are taken. These are the hostile forces, and against these man must contend. To them he opposes his intellect, his moral energy; he seeks to adapt himself to his place in the universe. He discovers that these foes are blind, not necessarily his enemies, if he can trace their path. If he can read the secret of their working, they cease to threaten him; he holds them with the reins of intellect, and binds them to his chariot, and behold like swift steeds they carry him whithersoever it pleases him, and on, on, they draw his car of progress. In this manner the sway of man's genius is extended on earth. Already life is far easier than it was among our ancestors ten thousand years ago; the epidemic is checked by wise sanitary regulations, greater justice prevails in government, and the means of happiness are extended over wider areas of the population. What we thus behold realized on a partial scale, we conceive in our visions of the future to be indefinitely prolonged, the course of development leading to higher and higher planes, healthier conditions, wiser laws, nobler manners. The moral order will thus increase on earth. The moral order never is, but is ever becoming. It grows with our growth, and to bring on the triumph of intellect over mechanism, of responsible morality over irresponsible force, is our mission. The purpose of man's life is not happiness, but worthiness. Happiness may come as an accessory, we dare never make it an end. There is that striving for the perfect within us: in it we live, by it we are exalted above the clod; it is the one and only solace that never fails us, and the experience of progress in the past, the hope of greater progress in the future, is the redeeming feature of life. But the condition of all progress is experience; we must go wrong a thousand times before we find the right. We struggle, and grope and injure ourselves until we learn the uses of things. Pain therefore becomes a necessity, but it acquires in this view a new and nobler meaning, for it is the price humanity pays for an invaluable good. Every painful sickness, every premature death, becomes the means of averting sickness and death hereafter. Every form of violence, every social wrong, every inmost tribulation, is the result of general causes and becomes a goad in the sides of mankind, pressing them on to correct the hoary abuses it has tolerated, the vicious principles of government, education and economy to which it has conformed. Wide as the earth is the martyrdom of man, but the cry of the martyr is the creaking of the wheel which warns us that the great car of human progress is in motion.

If we keep duly in mind the position which the human race occupies over against nature, we shall not accuse fate. Fate is our adversary; we must wrestle with it, we are here to establish the law of our own higher nature in defiance of fate. And this is the prerogative of man, that he need not blindly follow the law of his being, but that he is himself the author of the moral law, and creates it even in acting it out. We are all soldiers in the great army of mankind, battling in the cause of moral freedom; some to fight as captains, others to do valiant service in the ranks; some to shout the pæan of victory, others to fall on the battle field or to retire wounded or crippled to the rear. But as in every battle so too in this, the fallen and the wounded have a share in the victory; by their sufferings have they helped, and the greenest wreath belongs to them.

It is strictly in accordance with the view we have taken, that we behold in the performance of duty the solace of affliction. All of us have felt, after some great bereavement, the beneficent influence of mere labor: even the mechanical part of duty affords us some relief. The knowledge that something must be done calls us away from brooding over our griefs, and forces us back into the active currents of life. The cultivation of the intellect also is a part of man's duty, and stands us in great stead in times of trouble. We should seek to accustom the mind to the aspect of large interests. In the pursuit of knowledge there is nothing of the personal: into the calm and silent realm of thought the feelings can gain no entrance. There, after the first spasms of emotion have subsided, we may find at least a temporary relief,—there for hours we drink in a happy oblivion. But more is needed, and the discharge of the duties of the heart alone can really console the heart. There is this secret in the affections, that they constantly add to our strength. Constant communion between allied natures leads to their mutual enrichment by all that is best in either. But when the rude hand of death interferes, we are as a stream whose outlet is barred, as a creeper whose stay is broken. A larger channel is needed then into which the waters of our love may flow, a firm support, to which the tattered tendrils of affection may cling anew. True, the close and intimate bond that unites friend to friend can have no substitute, but the warm love that obtains in the personal relations may be expanded into a wider and impersonal love, which, if less intense, is broader, which, if less fond, is even more ennobling. The love you can no longer lavish on one, the many call for it. The cherishing care you can no longer bestow upon your child, the neglected children of the poor appeal for it; the sympathy you can no longer give your friend, the friendless cry for it. In alleviating the misery of others, your own misery will be alleviated, and in healing you will find that there is cure.

This remedy is suggested in an ancient legend related of the Buddha, the great Hindoo reformer, who was so deeply affected by the ills of human life.* There came to him one day a woman who had lost her only child. She was wild with grief, and with disconsolate sobs and cries called frantically on the prophet to give back her little one to life. The Buddha gazed on her long and with that tender sympathy which drew all hearts to him, said, "Go my daughter, get me a mustard seed from a house into which death has never entered, and I will do as thou hast bidden me." And the woman took up the dead child, and began her search. From house to house she went saying, "Give me a mustard seed, kind folk, a mustard seed for the

* We have ventured to offer this interpretation of the legend in an article published in the Atlantic Monthly for June, 1875, from which the account in the text is taken.

prophet to revive my child." And they gave her what she asked, and when she had taken it, she inquired whether all were gathered about the hearth, father and mother and the children ; but the people would shake their heads and sigh, and she would turn on her way sadder than before. And far as she wandered, in town and village, in the crowded thoroughfare, and by the lonely road side, she found not the house into which death had never entered. Then gradually as she went on, the meaning of the Buddha's words dawned upon her mind ; gradually as she learned to know the great sorrow of the race every where around her, her heart went out in great yearning sympathy to the companions of her sorrow ; the tears of her pity fell free and fast, and the passion of her grief was merged in compassion. She had learned the great lesson of renunciation ; had learned to sink self in the unselfish.

From the depths of the heart the stream of grief rises resistless, the dams and dykes of reason are impotent to stay its course. Prepare a channel therefore to lead out its swelling tide away to the great ocean of mankind's sorrow, where in commingling it shall be absorbed.

The consolations of the Ideal are vigorous : they do not encourage idle sentiment : they recommend to the sufferer, action. The loss indeed as we set out by saying, remains a loss, and no preaching or teaching can ever make it otherwise. The question is, whether it shall weaken and embitter us, or become the very purification of our souls, and lead us to grander and diviner deeds, lead us to raise unto the dead we mourn, a monument in our lives that shall be better than any pillared chapel or storied marble tomb.

Thus from whatever point we start, we arrive at the same conclusion still: "not in the creed but in the deed!" In the deed is the pledge of the sacredness of life; in the deed is the reward of our activities in health; in the deed our solace, and our salvation even in the abysmal gulfs of woe. In hours of great sorrow we turn in vain to nature for an inspiring thought. We question the sleepless stars; they are cold and distant: the winds blow, the rivers run their course, the seasons change; they are careless of man. In the world of men alone do we find an answering echo to the heart's needs. Let us grasp hands cordially and look into each other's eyes for sympathy, while we travel together on our road toward the unknown goal. To help one another is our wisdom, and our renown, and our sweet consolation.

VIII.

SPINOZA.

Two centuries have elapsed since Spinoza passed from the world of the living, and to-day that high and tranquil spirit walks the earth once more and men make wide their hearts to receive his memory and his name. The great men whom the past has wronged, receive at last time's tardy recompense.

On the day that Columbus set sail for America, the Jews left Spain in exile. Many of their number, however, who could not find it in their hearts to bid adieu to their native land, remained and simulated the practice of devout Catholics while in secret they preserved their allegiance to their ancestral religion. They occupied high places in the church and state, and monks, prelates and bishops were counted in their ranks. Ere long the suspicions of the Inquisition were alarmed against these covert heretics, and their position became daily more perilous and insecure. Some were condemned to the stake, others pined for years in dungeons; those that could find the means, escaped and sought in distant lands security and repose from persecution. It was especially the Free States of Holland whose enlightened policy offered an asylum to the fugitives, and thither accordingly in great numbers they directed their steps. Their frugality, their thrift and enterprise, contributed not a little to build up the prosperity of the Dutch metropolis.

In the opening of the seventeenth century a considerable congregation of the Jews had collected in the city of Amsterdam. There in the year 1632, the child of Spanish emigrants, Benedict Spinoza was born. Of his childhood we know little. At an early age he was initiated into the mysteries of Hebrew lore, was instructed in the Hebrew grammar, and learned to read and translate the various writings of the Old Testament. He was taught to thread his way through the mazes of the Talmud, and its subtle discussions proved an admirable discipline in preparing him for the favorite pursuits of his after years. Lastly he was introduced to the study of the Jewish philosophers, among whom Maimonides and Ibn Ezra engaged his especial attention. Maimonides, one of the most profound thinkers of the middle ages, strove to harmonize the teachings of Aristotle with the doctrines of the Bible. Ibn Ezra on the other hand, was a confirmed sceptic. In his biblical commentaries he anticipates many noteworthy discoveries of modern criticism, and his orthodoxy in other respects also is more than doubtful.

In all these different branches of theology the young Spinoza made rapid progress and soon gained astonishing proficiency. He was the favorite of his instructors, and they predicted that he would one day become a shining light of the synagogue. Not content, however, with this course of study, Spinoza addressed himself to the study of Roman literature, and with the assistance of a certain Dr. Van den Ende, who had at that time gained considerable repute as a teacher of liberal learning, he soon became an accomplished Latin scholar. He also took up the study of Geometry and of Physics, and acquired considerable skill in the art of sketching. His mind being thus stored with various knowledge, he was prepared to enter the vast realm of metaphysical speculation and here the works of Rene Déscartes, preëminently engaged his attention. Déscartes, whose motto, *De omnibus dubitandum est*, sufficiently indicates the revolutionary character of his teachings, was the leader of the new school of thought on the continent. His influence proved decisive in shaping the career of Spinoza. Bruno also deserves mention among those who determined the bias of Spinoza's mind. I mean that Bruno who was among the first followers of Copernicus, who proclaimed the doctrine of the infinity of worlds and who himself inculcated a species of pantheism for which he paid the last penalty at Rome in the year 1600, thirty-two years before Spinoza was born.

By all these influences the mind of the young philosopher was widened beyond the sphere of his early education. In the pursuit of truth he sought the society of congenial minds, and found among the cultivated Christians of his day that intellectual sympathy of which he stood in need. From the high plane of thought which he had now reached, the rites and practices of external religion dwindled in importance, and the questions of creed for which the mass of men contend appeared little and insignificant. His absence from the worship of the synagogue now began to be remarked; it was rumored that he neglected the prescribed fasts and he was openly charged with partaking of forbidden food. At first he was treated with great leniency. So high was his credit with the Rabbis, so impressed were they with his singular abilities, that they strove by every gentle means to win him back to his allegiance. They admonished him, held out prospects of honor and emolument; it is even stated that at last in despair of reclaiming him they offered an annual pension of a thousand florins to purchase his silence. Spinoza himself was keenly alive to the gravity of his position. It had been fondly hoped that he would shed new lustre upon the religion of Israel. He would be accused of vile ingratitude for deserting his people. He foresaw the inevitable rupture that would cut him off forever from friends and kinsmen, from the opportunities of wealth and honorable position, and deliver him over to privation and poverty. He himself tells us in the introduction of a work which had long been forgotten and has been only recently rescued from oblivion, that he saw riches and honor and all those goods for which men strive, placed before him on the one hand, and a sincere life serenely true to itself on the other; but that the former seemed veritable shams and evils compared with that one great good. Nay, he said, though he might never reach the absolute truth, he felt as one sick unto death, who knows but one balm that can help him and who must needs search for that balm whereby perchance he may be healed.

Great was the commotion stirred up against him in the Jewish community of Amsterdam. One evening a fanatic assaulted him on the street and attempted his life. The stroke of the assassin's dagger was successfully parried. But Spinoza felt that the city was now no longer safe for him to dwell in. He fled and for some time frequently changed his place of residence, until at last he settled at the Hague where he remained until his death. In the mean time the lenient spirit of the Jewish leaders had changed into stern, uncompromising rigor. Observe now how persecution breeds persecution. It had been the pride of Judaism from of old that within its pale the practice of religion was deemed more essential than the theory; that it permitted the widest divergence in matters of belief, and granted ample tolerance to all. But these Jews of Amsterdam, fresh from the dungeons and the torture chambers of the Inquisition, had themselves imbibed the dark spirit of their oppressors. Uriel d'Acosta they had driven to the verge of insanity and to a tragic death by their cruel bigotry. And now the same methods were employed against a wiser and greater and purer man, far than he.

On the 27th of July, 1656, in the synagogue of Amsterdam, the sacred ark, containing the scrolls of the law, being kept open during the ceremony, the edict of excommunication was solemnly promulgated. It reads somewhat as follows:

"By the decree of the angels and the verdict of the saints we separate, curse and imprecate Baruch de Spinoza with the consent of the blessed God and of this holy congregation, before the holy books of the Law with the commandments that are inscribed therein, with the ban with which Joshua banned Jericho, with the curse with which Elias cursed the youths, and with all the imprecations that are written in the Law. Cursed be he by day and cursed by night; cursed when he lies down, and cursed when he rises; cursed in his going forth, and cursed in his coming in. May the Lord God refuse to pardon him; may his wrath and anger be kindled against this man, and on him rest all the curses that are written in this book of the Law. May the Lord wipe out his name from under the heavens, and separate him for evil from all the tribes of Israel, with all the curses of the firmament that are written in the book of the Law. And ye that hold fast to the Lord God are all living this day! we warn you that none shall communicate with him either by word of mouth or letter, nor show him any favor, nor rest under the same roof with him, nor approach his person within four yards, nor read any writing that he has written."

When Spinoza heard of this anathema he calmly replied: "They compel me to do nothing which I was not previously resolved upon." He retired from the commerce of the world. He coveted solitude. Within his silent chamber he moved in a world of his own. There in twenty years of patient passionless toil he built up the mighty edifice of his system. It rises before us as if hewn of granite rock. Its simplicity, its grandeur, its structural power have been the wonder of men. I can offer only the barest outline of its design.

Man's questioning spirit seeks to penetrate to the heart of Nature, would grasp the origin of things. There is this mighty riddle: who will solve it? Various attempts have been made. Pantheism is one. Spinoza was the great philosopher of Pantheism.

Beneath all diversity there is unity. In all of Nature's myriad forms and changes, there is a substance unchangeable. It is uncreated, undivided, uncaused, the Absolute, Infinite, God. Thought and extension are its attributes; it is the One in All, the All in One. God is not matter, is not mind; is that deeper unity in which matter and mind are one; God or Nature, Spinoza says. This is not the God of theology. God is in the tree, in the stone, in the stars, in man. God does not live, nor labor for any purpose, but produces from the necessity of his Being in endless variety, in ceaseless activity. He is the inner cause of all things, the ultimate Reality, and all things are as in their nature they partake of him.

Man also is of God. The essence of man is in the mind. Man is a logical being. God alone owns truth; in so far as man thinks truly and clearly, he is a part of the infinite God. Logic is the basis of ethics. Spinoza ignores sentiment, ignores art. Good and evil are but other names for useful and not useful. But that alone is useful that we follow the necessary and universal laws, seeking by the depth and reach of intellect to know and understand.

Virtue is the pursuit of knowledge. There are three kinds of knowledge: the blurred perceptions of the senses, the light of the understanding, the intuition of intellect. The last is the highest.

Virtue is the sense of being; whatever heightens the joyous consciousness of our active faculties is therefore good. The wise man delights in the moderate enjoyment of pleasant food and drink, in the color and loveliness of green shrubs, in the adornment of garments, in music's sweetness. But our true being is to be found only in intellect; hence, virtue the joy of being, is the joy of thought; hence, the bold assertion—that is moral which helps, and that immoral which hinders thought.

Man is a social being. As a drop is raised upward in the great ocean by the onflowing of the wave, so the individual mind is exalted by the presence and communion of congenial minds moving in the same current.

'Tis thus that Spinoza deduces the social virtues. Hate is evil at all times, for hate implies the isolation and the weakness of the powers of reason. We should reward hatred with love and restore the broken accord of intellect. Love is the sense of kinship in the common search for reason's goal —wisdom. That all men should so live and act together that they may form, as it were, one body and one mind, is the ideal of life. Friendship therefore he prizes as the dearest of earth's possessions, and wedlock he esteems holy because in it is cemented the union of two souls for the common search of truth. We should be serene at all times and shun fear, which is weakness, and hope also which is the child of desire, and haughtiness and humbleness and remorse and pity should we avoid. But in stillness and with collected power shall we possess our souls obedient to the laws of mind that make our being and helping when we help for reason's sake. The passions bind us to passing phenomena. When they become transparent to our reason, when we know their causes then our nature conquers outward nature and we are masters, we are free.

Thus the emotional life is extinguished. The feelings lose their color and vitality, become blank "as lines and surfaces," and man, freed from the constraints of passion, dwells in the pure realm of intellect, and in constant intercourse with the mind of God, fulfills the purpose of his existence—to know and understand.

Against the blows of misfortune also reason steels us. Sorrow is but the lurking suspicion that all might have been otherwise. When we come to know that all things are by necessity. we shall find tranquillity in yielding to the inevitable. For so

God works by necessity. For all things are in his hands as clay in the hand of the potter, which the potter taketh and fashioneth therefrom vessels of diverse value, some to honor and some to disgrace. And none shall rebuke him, for all is by necessity.

When the body passes away the mind does not wholly perish, but something remains that is infinite, an eternal modus dwelling in the depths of the eternal mind. But though we knew not that something of the mind remained, yet were goodness and strength of soul to be sought for above all else. For who, foreseeing that he cannot always feed on healthy nourishment, would therefore sate himself with deadly poison? or who, though he knew that the mind is not immortal, would therefore lead an empty life, devoid of reason's good and guidance? The wisdom of the wise and the freedom of the free is not in the aspect of death but of life. Religion and piety lead us to follow the laws of necessity in the world where they are manifest, to dwell on the intellect of God, of God their fount and origin.

But I forbear to enter farther into this wonderful system. We see a giant wrestling with nature, seeking to wrest from her her secret. Mysterious nature baffles him and the riddle is still unread. That substance of which he speaks is no more than an abstraction of the mind whose reality in the outward world he has failed to prove. He has also erred in turning aside from the rich and manifold life of the emotions, for the emotions are not in themselves evil, they are the seminal principle of all virtue.

On pillars of intellect, Spinoza reared his system. Still, solemn, sublime like high mountains it towers upward, but is devoid of color and warmth, and even the momentary glow that now and then starts up in his writings, passes quickly away like the flush of evening that reddens the snowy summits of Alpine ranges.

Spinoza's name marks a lofty peak in human history. He was a true man; no man more fully lived his teachings. If he describes the pursuit of knowledge as the highest virtue, he was himself a noble example of tireless devotion in that pursuit. He was well versed in the natural sciences, skillful in the use of the microscope, and his contributions to the study of the inner life of man have earned him lasting recognition. Johannes Mueller, the distinguished physiologist, has included the third division of Spinoza's *Ethics* in his well known work on physiology.

Religion, however, was Spinoza's favorite theme, that religion which is free from all passionate longings and averse to superstition of whatever kind. He was among the first to hurl his mighty arguments against the infallible authority of the Bible, arguments that still command attention though two hundred years have since passed by. Miracles, he said, are past belief, the beauty of Cosmos is far more deserving of admiration than any so called miracle could possibly be. He demanded—this was a great and novel claim—that the methods of natural science be applied to the study of scripture, that the character of the age and local surroundings be considered in determining the meaning of each scriptural author. In brief that a natural history of the bible, so to speak, should be attempted. He claimed that the priesthood had falsified the very book which they professed to regard most holy. He denied the Mosaic authorship of the Pentateuch, and set forth in singularly clear and lucid language the discrepancies in which that work abounds. He closed the treatise in which these views are laid down—the Theologico-political Tract—with a magnificent plea for liberty of conscience and of speech. That state alone, he says, can be free and happy which rests on the freedom of the individual citizen. Where the right of free utterance is curtailed, hypocrisy and shameful conformance flourish, and public contumely and disgrace which ought to serve as a mete punishment for the vicious, become a halo about the head of the most noble of men. Religion and piety, he concludes, the state has a right to demand, but nothing hereafter shall be known as religion and piety save the practice of equity and of a wise and helpful love.

It was a bold awakening note which thus rang out into the seventeenth century, and theologians were bitter in their replies. The book was confiscated and Christian curses were added to Jewish anathemas. But they failed to affect Spinoza.

Few men have suffered as he did. Few have preserved the same equanimity of soul in the face of adverse fortune. Twenty years he dwelt alone. For days he did not leave his student's closet, drawing his mighty circles, intent on those high thoughts that formed the companionship he loved. Those that knew him well revered him. De Witt the noble statesman, De Witt who ended his days so miserably, torn to pieces by a maddened mob, sought his counsel. Young ardent disciples from a distance sent him words of cheer into his solitude. His soul was pure as sunlight, his character crystal clear. He was frugal in the extreme: a few pence a day sufficed to sustain him. Not that he affected austere views in general, but the deep meditations that occupied his mind left him little time or inclination for the grosser pleasures. His sense of honor was scrupulously nice. Again and again did he reject the munificent pensions which his friends pressed upon him; he would be free and self-sustained in all things. In his leisure hours he busied himself with the grinding and polishing of optical lenses, an exercise that offered him at once the means of support and a welcome relaxation from the severe strain of mental effort. His temper was rarely ruffled; he was placid, genial, childlike. When wearied with his labors he would descend to the family of his landlord, the painter Van der Speke, and entering into the affairs of these simple people, he found, in their unaffected converse, the relief he sought.

He valued the peace of mind which he had purchased so dearly. When the Elector of the Palatinate offered him the chair of philosophy at the University of Heidelberg on condition that he would so expound his philosophy as not to interfere with the established religion, he declined, replying that he could teach the truth only as he saw it, and that evil and designing men would doubtless add point and poison to his words. Yet he was fearless. When toward the close of his career, his life was again imperiled, the grave tranquillity of his demeanor inspired his agitated friends with calmness and confidence.

He had gained his forty-fourth year. For half a life time he had been fighting a treacherous disease, that preyed in secret upon his health. His life was slowly ebbing away amidst constant suffering, yet no complaint crossed his lips and his nearest companions were hardly aware of what he endured. In the early part of the year 1677 one day in February, while the family of the painter were at church the end approached. Only a single friend was with him. Calmly as he had lived, in the stillness of the Sunday afternoon, Spinoza passed away.

He has left a name in history that will not fade. His people cast him out, Christianity rejected him, but he has found a wider fellowship, he belongs to all mankind. Great hearts have throbbed responsive to his teachings and many a sorrowful soul has owned the restful influence of his words. He was a helper of mankind. Not surely because he solved the ultimate problems of existence—what mortal ever will—but because he was wise in the secret of the heart, because he taught men to appease their fretful passions in the aspect of the infinite laws in which we live and are.

Sacred is the hour in which we read his Ethics. From the heat and glare of life we enter into its precincts as into the cool interior of some hallowed temple of religion. But no idol stands there; the spirit of truth alone presides and sanctifies the place and us. The great men of the past we will reverence. They are mile-stones on the highway of humanity, types of the Infinite, that has dawned in human breasts. Such an one was he of whom I have spoken. And more and more as the light increases among men will all that was good and great in him shine forth to irradiate their path. And as we stand here to-day on this day of remembrance to recall his teachings and his example, so when other centuries shall have elapsed, the memory of Spinoza will still live, posterity will still own him, and distant generations will name him anew: Benedictus—Blessed!

IX.

THE FOUNDER OF CHRISTIANITY*

"I am not come to destroy, but to fulfil, for verily I say unto you till heaven and earth pass away one jot or one tittle shall in no wise pass from the law till all be fulfilled." "Resist not evil, * * * bless them that curse you, do good to them that hate you."

In these sayings of Jesus the key note of early Christianity is struck. It was not a revolt against Judaism, it was but a reiterated assertion of what other and older Prophets of the Hebrews had so often and so fervently preached. The law was to remain intact, but the spiritual law was meant, the deeper law of conscience that underlies the forms of legislation and the symbols of external worship.

There is a rare and gracious quality in the personality of Jesus as described in the Gospels, which has exercised its charm upon the most heterogeneous nations and periods of history wide apart in the order of time and of culture.

To grasp the subtle essence of that charm, and thereby to understand what it was that has given

* A discourse delivered on Sunday, December 31, 1876.

Christianity so powerful a hold upon the affections of mankind, were a task well worthy the attention of thoughtful minds. We desire to approach our subject in the spirit of reverence that befits a theme with which the tenderest fibres of faith are so intimately interwoven; at the same time we shall pay no regard to the dogmatic character with which his later followers have invested Jesus, for we behold his true grandeur in the pure and noble humanity which he illustrated in his life and teachings.

The New Testament presents but scant material for the biography of Jesus, and the authenticity, even of the little that remains to us, has been rendered extremely uncertain by the labors of modern critics. A few leading narratives, however, are doubtless trustworthy, and these will suffice for our purpose. A brief introduction on the character of the people among whom the new prophet arose, the characteristics of the age in which he lived, and the beliefs that obtained in his immediate surroundings, will assist us in our task.

The expectation of the Messiah had long been rife among the Jews. Holding themselves to be the elect people of God, they believed the triumph of monotheism to be dependent upon themselves. The prophets of Jehovah had repeatedly assured them that their supremacy would finally be acknowledged. Events however had turned out differently. Instead of success they met with constant defeat and disaster; Persia, Egypt, Syria had successively held their land in subjection; the very existence of their religion was threatened, and the heathen world, far from showing signs of approaching conversion, insisted upon its errors with increased obstinacy and assurance. And yet Jehovah had distinctly promised that he would raise up in his own good time, a new ruler from the ancient line of Israel's Kings, a son of David, who should lead the people to Victory. To his sceptre all the nations would bow, and in his reign the faith of the Hebrews would be acknowledged as the universal religion. Every natural means for the fulfilment of these predictions seemed now cut off, nothing remained but to take refuge in the supernatural; it was said that the old order of things must entirely pass away; a new heaven and a new earth be created and what was called the Kingdom of Heaven might then be expected. The "Kingdom of Heaven," a phrase that frequently recurs in the literature of the Jews, is used, not to describe a locality, but to denote a state of affairs on earth, in which the will of heaven would be generally obeyed without the further intervention of human laws and government. The agency of the Messiah was looked to, for the consummation of these happy hopes. To reward those who had perished before his coming, many moreover of those that slept in the dust would awaken, and the general resurrection of the dead would signalize the approach of the millennium.

At the end of the first century B. C. these expectations had created a wild ferment among the population of Palestine. Now if ever, it was fondly urged, they must be fulfilled. The need was at its highest, help then must be nighest. For matters had indeed grown from bad to worse, the political situation was intolerable, after the brief spell of independence in the days of the Maccabees, the Roman yoke had been fastened upon the necks of the people, and the weight of oppression became tenfold more difficult to support from the sweet taste of liberty that had preceded it. The rapacity of the Roman Governors knew no bounds. A land impoverished by incessant wars and the frequent failure of the crops, was drained of its last resources to satisfy the enormous exactions of a foreign despot, while to all this was added the humiliating consciousness that it was a nation of idolators which was thus permitted to grind the chosen people.

Nor was the condition of religion at all more satisfactory. It is true the splendid rites of the public worship were still maintained at the Temple, and Herod was even then re-building the Sanctuary on a scale of unparalleled magnificence. Bright was the sheen and glitter of gold upon its portals, solemn the ceremonies enacted in its halls, and grand and impressive the voices of the Levitic choirs as they sang to the tuneful melody of cymbals and of harps. But the lessons of history teach us that the times in which lavish sums are expended on externals, are not usually those in which religion posesses true vitality and power and depth. Here was a brand flickering near extinction; here was a builder who built for destruction; the Temple had ceased to satisfy the needs of the people.

In the cities an attempt to supply the deficiency was made by the party of the Pharisees. They sought to broaden and to spiritualize the meaning of scripture—they laid down new forms of religious observance by means of which every educated man became, so to speak, his own priest. The religion of the Pharisees however assumed a not inconsiderable degree of intellectual ability on the part of its followers. So far as it went it answered very well for the intelligent middle classes. But out in the country districts it did not answer at all; not for the herdsmen, not for the poor peasants, not for those who had not even the rudiments of learning and who could do nothing with a learned religion. And yet these very men before all others needed something to support them, something to cling to, even because they were so miserably poor and illiterate. They did not get what they wanted—

they felt very strongly that the burdens upon them were exceedingly grievous; that while they suffered and starved, religion dwelt in palaces, and had no heart for their misfortunes. They felt that something was wrong and rotten in the then state of affairs, and that a new state must come, and a heaven-sent king, who would lend a voice to their needs, and lift them with strong arms from out their despair and degradation. Nowhere was this feeling more marked than in the district of Galilee. A beautiful land with green, grassy valleys, groves of sycamores, broad blue lakes, and villages nestling picturesquely on the mountain slopes, it nourished an ardent and impulsive population. Their impatience with the existing order of things had already found vent in furious revolt. Judah, their famous leader, had perished; his two sons, James and Simon, had been nailed to the cross; the Messiah was daily and hourly expected; various impostors successively arose and quickly disappeared; when would the hour of deliverance come; when would the true Messiah appear at last?

It was at such a time and among such a people, that there arose Jesus of Nazareth in Galilee. What was the startling truth he taught? What was the new revelation he preached to the sons of men? An old truth, and an old sermon—Righteousness; no more, meaning nothing at all, a mere trite common-place, on the lips of the time-server and the plausible vendor of moral phrases. Meaning mighty changes for the better, when invoked with a profounder sense of its sanctity, and a new sacredness in life, and larger impulses for ever and for ever. Righteousness he taught, and the change that was to come by righteousness. Yes, so deep was his conviction, so profoundly had the current conceptions of the day affected him, that he believed the change to be near at hand, that he himself might be its author, himself Messiah.

The novelty of Jesus' work has been sought in various directions. It has been said, for instance, to consist in the overthrow of phariseeism; and it is true that he rebukes the pharisees in the most severe terms; these reproaches, however, were not directed against the party as a whole, but only against its more extravagant and unworthy members. The pharisees were certainly not a "race of hypocrites, and a generation of vipers." Let us remember that Jesus himself, in the main, adhered to their principles; that his words often tally strictly with theirs; that even the golden sayings which are collected in the sermon on the mount, may be found in the contemporaneous Hebrew writings, whose authors were pharisees. Thirty years before his time, Hillel arose among the pharisees, renowned for his marvellous erudition, beloved and revered because of the gentleness and kindliness of his bearing, the meekness with which he endured persecution, the loving patience with which he overcame malice and hate. When asked to express in brief terms the essence of the law, he to the pharisee replied, "Do not unto others what thou wouldst not that others do unto thee; this is the essence, all the rest is commentary,—go and learn." Jesus fully admits the authority of the pharisees. "The pharisees," he says, "sit in Moses' seat; all therefore whatsoever they bid you observe, that observe and do." If we read the gospel of Matthew, we find that he does not attempt to abrogate the pharisaic commandments, but only insists upon the greater importance of the commandments of the heart. "Woe," he cries, "for ye pay tithe of mint, of anise and cumin, but ye have omitted the weightier matters of the law, judgment, mercy and faith, these ought ye to have done, *and not to leave the other undone*,"—and again, "If thou bring thy gift to the altar, and there rememberest that thy brother hath aught against thee, leave there thy gift before the altar and go thy way; first be reconciled to thy brother, and then *come and offer thy gift*." The leper also whom he cured of his disease, he advises to bring the gift prescribed by the Jewish ritual. We cannot fully understand the conduct of Jesus in this respect, unless we bear in mind that he believed the millenial time to be near at hand. At that time it was supposed the ancient ceremonial of Judaism would come to an end by its own limitation; until that time arrived, it should be respected. He does not wage war against the religious tenets and practices of his age; only when they interfere with the superior claims of moral rectitude does he bitterly denounce them, and ever insists that righteousness be recognized as the one thing above all others needful.

Nor is the novelty of Jesus' work to be found in the extension of the gospel to the heathen world. It seems, on the contrary, highly probable that he conceived his mission to lie within the sphere of his own people, and devoted his chief care and solicitude to their welfare. "I am not sent but unto the lost sheep of the house of Israel," he says; and thus he charges his apostles, "Go ye not into the way of the Gentiles, and into any city of the Samaritans enter ye not. Go rather to the lost sheep of the house of Israel, and as ye go, preach, saying the kingdom of heaven is at hand." And yet his exclusive devotion to the interest of the Jews is not at variance with the world-embracing influence attributed to the Messianic character. In common with all his people, he believed that upon the approach of the millennium, the nations of the earth would come of their own accord, to the holy mount of Israel, accept Israel's religion, and thenceforth live obedient to the Messianic King. The millennium was now believed to be actually in sight. "Verily I say unto you there be some standing here who shall not taste of death until they see the Son of man coming in his Kingdom." From the Jewish standpoint, therefore, which was the one taken by Jesus and the earliest Christians, the mission to the heathen was unnecessary.

"And again it has been said that the evangel of Jesus was new, in that it substituted for the stern law of retribution the methods of charity and the law of love; that while the elder prophets had taught the people to consider themselves servants of a task-master, he taught them freedom and brotherhood. But is this true? Will any one who has read the Hebrew Prophets with attention, venture to assert that they instil a slavish fear into the hearts of men; they whose every line speaks aspiration, whose every word breathes liberty? It is true their language is often stern when they dwell on duty. And it is right that it should be so, for so also is duty stern and in matters of conscience sentimentalism is out of place, harmful. Simple obedience to the dictates of the moral law is required, imperatively, unconditionally, not for pity's sake, nor for love's sake, but for the right's sake, simply and solely because it is right. But the emotions that are never the sufficient sanctions of conduct may ennoble and glorify right conduct. And how tenderly do the ancient prophets also attune their monitions to the promptings of the richest and purest of human sympathies. "Thy neighbor thou shalt love as thyself," was written by them, and "Have we not all one Father, has not one God created us all." Thy poor brother too is thy brother, and in secret shalt thou give charity. In the dusk of the evening the poor are to come into the cornfields and gather there, and no man shall know who has given and who has received. The ancient prophets were idealists, preachers of the Spirit as opposed to the form that cramps and belittles. In Jesus we behold a renewal of their order, a living protest against the formalism that had in the interval become encrusted about their teachings, only differing from his predecessors in this, that the hopes which they held out for a distant future, seemed to him nigh their fulfilment, and that he believed himself destined to fulfil them.

If we can discover nothing that had not been previously stated in the substance of Jesus' teachings, there is that in the method he pursued, which calls for genuine admiration and reverence, the method of rousing against the offender the better nature in himself: of seeming yielding to offence based on an implicit trust in the resilient energy of the good; of conquering others, by the strength of meekness and the might of love. Hillel too was endowed with this strength of meekness, and Buddha had said, long before the days of Jesus : " Hatred is not conquered by hatred at any time, hatred is conquered by love ; this is an old rule." But in the story of no other life has this method been applied with such singular sweetness, with such consistent harmony from the beginning to the end. Whether we find him in the intimate circle of his disciples, whether he is instructing the multitude along the sunny shores of Lake Gennesareth, whether he stands before the tribunal of his judges, or in the last dire agonies of death—he is ever the patient man, the loving teacher, the man of sorrows, who looks beyond men and their crimes to an ideal humanity, and confides in that ; who gives largely, and forgives even because he gives so much.

But we shall not touch the true secret of his power until we recall his sympathy with the neglected classes of society; that quality of his nature which caused the poor of Galilee to hail him as their deliverer, which produced so lasting an impression upon his contemporaries, and made the development of his doctrines into a great religion possible. His gospel was preëminently the gospel for the poor : he sat down with despised publicans, he did not shun the contamination of lepers, nay nor of the moral leprosy of sin—he visited the hovels of paupers and taught his disciples to prefer them to the mansions of the fortunate; he applied himself with peculiar fervor to those dumb illiterate masses of Galilee, who knew not whither they might turn, to what they might cling. He gave them hope, he brought them help. And so it came about that in the early Christian communities which were still fresh from the presence of the master, the appeal to conscience he had made so powerfully, resulted in solid helpfulness; so it came about that in those pristine days, the Church was a real instrument of practical good, with few forms, and little parade, but with love feasts and the communion table spread with repasts for the needy. "Come unto me all ye that labor and are heavy laden and I will give you rest. Take my yoke upon you and learn of me, * * for my yoke is easy and my burden is light."

It is from such particulars that there was drawn that fascinating image which has captivated the fancy and attracted the worship of mankind. The image of the pale man with the deep, earnest eyes, who roused men to new exertions for the good, who lifted up the down-trodden, who loved little children and taught the older children in riddles and parables that they might understand, and the brief career of whose life was hallowed all the more in memory, because of the mournful tragedy in which it closed. All the noblest qualities of humanity were put into this picture and made it lovely. It was the humanity, not the dogma of Jesus, by which Christianity triumphed. Like a refreshing shower in the perfumed spring, his glad tidings of a new enthusiasm for the good came upon the arid Roman world, sickening with the dry rot of self-indulgence, and thirsting for some principle to give a purpose to the empty weariness of existence. Like a message from a sphere of light it spread to the Germanic tribes, tempered the harshness of their manners, taught them a higher law than that of force, and conquered their grim strength with the mild pleadings of the Master of meekness in far-off Galilee.

It is the moral element contained in it that alone gives value and dignity to any religion, and only then when its teachings serve to stimulate and purify our aspirations toward the good, does it deserve to retain its ascendancy over mankind. Claiming to be of celestial origin, the religions have drawn their secret spell from the human heart itself. There is a principle of reverence inborn in every child of man,—this he would utter. He sees the firmament above him, with its untold hosts; he stands in the midst of mighty workings, he is filled with awe; he stretches forth his arms to grasp the Infinite which his soul seeketh, he makes unto himself signs and symbols, saying, let these be tokens of what no words can convey. But a little time elapses, and these symbols themselves seem more than human, they point no more beyond themselves, and man becomes an idolator, not of stone and wood merely. Then it is needful that he remember the divine power with which his soul has been clothed from the beginning, that by the force of some moral impulse he may break through the fetters of the creeds, and cast aside the weight of doctrines that express his best ideals no more. And so we find in history that every great religious reformation has been indebted for its triumphs, not to the doctrines that swam upon the surface, but to the swelling currents of moral energy that stirred it from below; not to the doctrine of the Logos in Jesus' day, but to the tidings of release which he brought to the oppressed, not to "justification by faith," in Luther's time, but to the mighty reaction to which his thunderous protest lent a voice, against the lewdness and the license of a corrupt and cankerous priesthood. The appeal to conscience has ever been the lever that raised mankind to a higher plane of religion.

Conscience, righteousness, what is there new in these—their maxims are as old as the hills? Truly, and as barren often as the rocks. The novelty of righteousness is not in itself, but in its novel application to the particular unrighteousness of a particular age. It was thus that Jesus applied to the sins and mock sanctities of his day, the ancient truths known to the prophets and to others long before him. It is thus that every new reformer will seek to bring home to the men of his generation what it is that the ancient standard of right and justice now requires at their hands. That all men are brothers, who did not concede it? But that the enslaved man too is our brother, what a convulsion did that not cause, what vast expenditure of blood and treasure until that was made plain. That we should relieve the necessities of the poor, who will deny it? But that a social system which year by year witnesses the increase of the pauper class, and the increase of their miseries, stands condemned before the tribunal of Religion, of justice, how long will it take before that is understood and taken to heart? The facts of righteousness are few and simple, but to apply them how mighty, how difficult a task. The time is approaching when this stupendous work must be attempted anew, and we, a small phalanx in the army of progress, would aid, with what power in us resides. Let this inspire us that we have the loftiest cause of the age for our own, that we are helping to pave the way for a stronger and freer and happier race. For by so laboring, alone can we feel that our life has a meaning under the sky and the sacred stars.

The year in which we have entered upon our

journey is passing away. To-night when the midnight bells send forth their clamorous voices, we shall greet the new year, and the work it brings. No peaceful task dare we expect, but something of good accomplished may it see.

> "Ring out wild bells to the wild sky,
> The flying cloud, the frosty light,
> The year is dying in the night,
> Ring out wild bells and let him die.
>
> "Ring out the old, ring in the new,
> Ring happy bells across the snow,
> The year is going, let him go,
> Ring out the false, ring in the true."

X.

THE FIRST ANNIVERSARY DISCOURSE.

It is May, the gladdest season of the year. Life is in the breezes, life in the vernal glory of the fields, life in the earth and in the skies. Of old, men were wont to go forth at this time into the forest, to wreath the fountains with garlands, to cover their houses with green branches, with songs and dances to celebrate the triumph of the Spring. Happy festivals, happy omens.

A year has now passed since we began our work, and for many months we have met in this hall week after week. We have reached the first resting place upon our journey, and it behooves us to look back once more upon the path we have travelled; and forward into the yet untried future that awaits us.

What was it that induced us to enter upon so perilous and for many reasons so uncertain an enterprise?

We felt a great need. Religion which ought to stand for the highest truth, had ceased to be true to us. We saw it at war with the highest intelligence of the day; religion and conscience also seemed no longer inseparably connected, as they should be. We saw that millions are annually lavished upon the mere luxuries of religion, gorgeous temples, churches and on the elaborate apparatus of salvation; we could not but reflect that if one tithe of the sums thus set apart were judiciously expended upon the wants of the many who are famishing, distress might often be relieved, sickness averted, and crime confined within more narrow boundaries. We saw around us many who had lapsed from their ancient faith but still preserved the outward show of conformance, encouraged in so equivocal a course, by the advice and example of noted leaders in the churches themselves. We saw that the great tides of being are everywhere sweeping mankind on to larger achievements than were known to the past; only within the churches all is still and motionless; only within the churches the obsolete forms of centuries ago are retained, or if concessions to the present are made, they are tardy, ungracious and insufficient. We beheld that the essentials of religion are neglected, even while its accessories are observed with greater punctiliousness than ever.

We were passing moreover through a period of momentous import in our country's history. The nation had just entered upon the second century of its existence, and the great recollections of what the fathers had done and designed for the republic, were fresh in our minds. We recalled the memorable words of Washington in his first inaugural address: " That the national policy would be laid in the pure and immutable principles of private morality." But we were startled to observe how greatly recent events had falsified these hopes and felt it our duty, within our own limited sphere, to restore something of that noble simplicity, something of that high fidelity to righteousness which it is said adorned the earlier days, and on which alone the fortunes of the state can rest securely hereafter.

Then also the question, how best to educate the children to a worthy life, confronted us. The doctrines of religion as commonly interpreted, we could no longer impart to them ; did we attempt to do so, they would be likely to discard them in later years, and would in the mean time be seriously injured in their moral estate by the struggle and its probable issue. On the other hand we were aware that the temptations which surround the young in this complex and highly wrought civilization of ours, are peculiarly dangerous and alluring, and by all the holiest instincts of humanity, we conceived ourselves bound to provide more effectively for their moral welfare. A few of us therefore took counsel how these objects might be attained, and we determined to take a step in a new direction. We did not conceal from ourselves the difficulties that would attend what we were about to undertake. We might expect honest opposition. There would be no need to shrink from that. We might expect misconstruction, unintentioned or with malice aforethought; we might expect also cold comfort from those illiberal liberals, who are eager enough to assert the principles of freedom for themselves, but relax alike their principles and their tempers when the limits are transcended which they have themselves reached, and which, on this account, they arbitrarily set up as the barriers of future progress. There were other obstacles inherent in the nature of the work itself. But all these weighed lightly in the scales, when opposed to the stern conviction, that there are certain hideous shams allowed to flourish in our public life; that there are certain great truths which ought to be brought home with new energy to the conscience of the people.

Upon what platform could we unite. To formulate a new creed was out of the question. However comprehensive in its statements it might be, nay though it had been the creed of absolute negation, from which indeed we are far removed, it would never have combined our efforts in permanent union. And yet it was plain that to be strong and to exert influence, we must effect a firm, cordial, enthusiastic agreement upon some great principle. The weakness of the Liberal Party had hitherto been, as we knew, its dread of organization. It ensured thereby for its members a greater measure of freedom than is elsewhere known, but it purchased this advantage at an immense expense of practical influence and coherency. Its forces are scattered, and in every emergency, it finds itself paralyzed for want of unity in its own ranks. The Catholic Church has pursued the opposite policy, and presents the most notable instance of its successful prosecution. It is so formidable, mainly because of its splendid scheme of organization, and the high executive ability of its leaders. But its power is maintained at a complete sacrifice of freedom. Could we not secure both? Could we not be free and strong? This was the problem before us, and it seemed to us we could.

What the exigencies of the modern age demand, more than aught else, is a new movement for the moral elevation of the race. Now the basic facts of man's moral nature, though insufficiently illustrated in practice, are universally admitted among civilized human beings. Concerning them there is and can be no dispute. Here then appeared the solid principle of our union. The moral ideal would point the way of safety, the moral ideal would permit us to preserve the sacred right of individual differences intact, and yet to combine with our fellow-men for the loftiest and purest ends. Taking the term creed therefore in its widest application, we started out with the watchword, Diversity in the Creed, Unanimity in the Deed. This feature, if any at all, lends character to our movement, and by it would we be judged. We claim to be thereby distinguished, as well from those religious corporations that base their organization upon definite theological dogmas, as also from the great majority of Liberals who meet for purposes of contemplation and poetical aspiration, in that we put the moral element prominently forward and behold in it the bond of our union, the pledge of our vitality.

But at the very threshold of our enterprise, we were met by the objection that our main premise is false; that morality is impossible without dogma, and that in neglecting the one we were virtually neutralizing our efforts toward the other. It became our first and most serious task therefore to show the futility of this objection, and to make clear by an appeal to philosophy and history that the claims of dogma are conditional, while the dictates of morality are imperative. Then, having established the priority and supremacy of the moral law, to examine what manner of substitute the ethical ideal can offer us to replace the offices of the doctrinal religions; what are the hopes it holds out, what its consolations, what it can give us for the priesthood and the church. With this task we have been occupied during the year that has gone by, and now, at the close, we propose to review once more, the chief steps which we have taken in the course of our enquiry.

We discussed in the first place the doctrine of immortality, and some of the main arguments upon which it is commonly founded.

We next proceeded to take up the study of the Hebrew Bible; for it is evident that so long as this book is clothed with infallible authority, arguments based on fact and logic avail nothing, and reason is helpless before any random scriptural quotation. We examined the composition of the work: we learned that many of those portions that are esteemed most ancient, are of comparatively recent origin; that the text is studded with discrepancies, and that the marks of savage and cruel customs such as the offering of human sacrifices to the Deity, are still clearly indented on the sacred volume. The conclusion followed that a book so full of contradiction, so deeply tinged with the evidence of human fallibility, could not have been the work of a divine author. The inspiration theory being thus divested of its support, we considered how baneful had been its influence on the course of human history; how it had retarded the progress of the Jews among whom it arose; how it had checked the intellectual development of Europe, how it had hampered the advancement of science; how it had offered a specious plea for the despotism of kings, and of the holy Inquisition; how in our own days it had become in the hands of the Southern slaveholders a most formidable means of perpetuating their infamous scheme of oppression. We concluded that whatever is false and worthless in the book we should feel at liberty to reject, while what is great and holy would not therefore become less great or less holy to us, because it was proven to be man's work, man's testimony to the divine possibilities inherent in the human soul.

We went on striving to penetrate more deeply the origin of that mysterious power which we call religion. To us it appeared that the feeling of the sublime is the root of the religious sentiment in man. That the Vedahs, Avesta, Koran, Bible are the songs of the nations on the theme of the infinite; and that the moral ideal, whether we endow it with personality or not, presents to us the highest type of sublimity and is the sole object worthy of religious reverence.

> "Who dare express him
> And who profess him
> Saying, 'I believe in him?'
> Who feeling, seeing, deny his being
> Saying I believe him not?

> "Call it then what thou wilt
> Call it bliss, heart, love, God;
> I have no name to give it.
> Feeling is all in all,
> The name is sound and smoke."

THE FIRST ANNIVERSARY DISCOURSE.

We maintained lastly, that the entrance of the moral into the sphere of religion has endowed the latter with whatever excellence it now possesses.

We showed in another course of lectures, that every great religious movement has been in the essence, a protest against the formalism and mock holiness of its time, and derived its vital impulses from the moral elements with which it was suffused. We instanced the case of monotheism, which, as we believe, arose in the struggle of the prophets against the immoral rites of Baal: We mentioned Buddha, the reformer of the Hindoos, whose sermon of unselfishness won for him the affections of the people. We referred on frequent occasions to the fact that Christianity likewise triumphed because of the humanity of Jesus: because he was the Master of meekness; because his gospel was a gospel for the poor. The result of all which was to confirm the priority of morality, and to show that it is indeed the source of whatever is durable and valuable in the Creeds.

Toward the end of February the two hundredth anniversary of the death of Benedict Spinoza, afforded us a welcome opportunity to dwell upon the life and philosophy of that illustrious thinker.

Later on, we endeavored to comprehend the causes which have produced that remarkable change the religious opinions of modern men, that is daily becoming more widely apparent. We found them to be the critical investigation of the Bible, the progress of the natural sciences, and indirectly, the influence of commerce and of industry. We attempted to set forth how the introduction of machinery became the means of fostering the growth of scepticism even among those classes to whom the arguments of scholars and men of science do not appeal. We spoke of the enlightenment of the masses, and considered the theory of those who hold that a religion, even when it is found to be false, should still be maintained as a salutary curb upon the passions of the multitude. We insisted that this view of religion is as unsound as it is degrading; that while all men may not be capable of the highest order of intellectual action, all men are capable of heart goodness, and goodness is the better part of religion; that a generous confidence is the highest principle of education, and that to trust men is the surest means of leading them to respond to our confidence; that we should cease therefore to preach the depravity of human nature and preach rather the grandeur which is possible to human nature; that in freedom alone can we become worthy of being free.

And again in a distinct group of lectures we sought to unfold our conception of the New Ideal, and to point out that which distinguishes it from

THE FIRST ANNIVERSARY DISCOURSE. 177

what has gone before. We spoke of its appeal to the higher nature, of its teachings concerning the Infinite within ourselves. We spoke of the priests that shall do its service; of the solace it affords us by its summons to larger duties; of the ethical schools that shall be erected for its culture; of the manner in which women may be prepared to aid in its propaganda; lastly of the form which it may assume in the future, in our discourse on the Order of the Ideal.

Thus far have we proceeded. We issued our appeal, at first, as men uncertain what the fortunes of their enterprise might be. But while we avowed it to be an experiment, we were deeply convinced that it was an experiment which deserved to be tried. And more and more as week followed week, the response from your side came back full and cordial; and more and more as the scope and the ultimate tendencies of our work were developed, new friends came to us whom we had not known, and it became apparent that there is a deep, downright purpose in your midst which will form a bond of union for us that shall not easily be snapped asunder. Until at last after a period had gone by, you thought it time to exchange your temporary organization for one more stable, and you declared to all who might be interested in learning it, that it is your intention and your hope to become a permanent institution in this community.

We have made a beginning only. If we look ahead, dangers and difficulties still lie thickly on our path. The larger work is still before us. But we will confide in the goodness of our cause, and believe that if it be good indeed, in the end it must succeed.

The country in which we live is most favorable for such experiments as ours. There are lands of older culture, and men there of wider vision and maturer wisdom, but nowhere, as in America, is a truth once seen, so readily applied, nowhere do even the common order of men so feel the responsibility for what transpires, and the impulse to see the best accomplished. Here no heavy hand of rulers crushes the incipient good. When the Pilgrims set out on their voyage across the unknown Atlantic, Robinson, their pastor, their leader, addressed them once more before they embarked, and in that solemn hour of parting, warned them against the self-sufficiency of a false conservatism, and dedicated them and the new states they might found, to the increase and the service of larger truths. To larger truths America is dedicated.

O, if it were thine, America, America that hast given political liberty to the world, to give that spiritual liberty for which we pant, to break also those spiritual fetters that load thy sons and daughters! All over this land thousands are searching and struggling for the better, they know not what. Oh that we might aid them in the struggle, and they us; and the hearts of many be knit together once more in a common purpose that would lift them above their sordid, weary cares, and ennoble their lives and make them glorious! The crops are waiting; may the reapers come!

APPENDIX.

APPENDIX.

I.

THE EVOLUTION OF HEBREW RELIGION.

"Dans l'opinion du peuple pour qui ces livres ont été écrits le point capital et essentiel n'est certes pas la narration historique, mais bien la législation et l'édification religieuse."[1]

In 1795, Frederick Augustus Wolf published a modest octavo volume entitled "Prolegomena to Homer," from whose appearance is dated the beginning of a new era of historic criticism. The composition of the poems of Homer formed its subject. For wellnigh twenty years the author had collected evidence, weighed arguments, and patiently tested his results by constant revision. His own wishes were engaged on the side of the unity of the great Grecian epic. But the results of his researches continued to point in the opposite direction, and at last his earnest devotion to truth compelled him to adopt a theory the soundness of whose construction seemed to be no longer questionable. He was thus worthy to become the "founder of the science of philology in its present significance."[2]

The influence of Wolf's discovery was not confined to the study of classic literature only. It quickly radiated through every department of history. "In every singing age," he said, "a single sæculum is almost like a single man. It is all one mind,

[1] "In the estimation of the people for whom these books were written, the capital, essential point surely was, not the historic narrative, but rather legislation and religious edification." (Nöldeke, 'Histoire Littéraire de l'Ancien Testament," p. 19.)

[2] Bonitz, "Ueber den Ursprung der Homerischen Gedichte," p. 11.

one soul."[1] This conception involved a new social law, and radically altered the current opinions concerning the relation of individual effort to the larger forces that affect the development of nations. The creative energy of remarkable minds was not, indeed, lessened in importance, but spontaneity, in this connection, acquired a new meaning ; and for the *Deus ex machina* of the olden time was substituted the cumulative force of centuries of progressive advancement, culminating, it is true, at last in the triumphant synthesis of genius. The commotion which the Wolfian theory has stirred up in the literary world is largely due to the wide range of ideas which it affected. Yet it was itself but a part of that general movement which, toward the close of the last century, became conspicuous in its effects on every field of human inquiry. Everywhere the shackles of authority were thrown off, and, in place of blindly accepting the testimony of the past, men turned to investigate for themselves. A new principle of research was everywhere acknowledged, a new method was created, and science, natural and historical, entered upon that astonishing career of discovery whose rich promise for the future we have but begun to anticipate.[2]

To the impetus given by Wolf, and to the new-born spirit of science which he carried into the sphere of philology, we owe among other valuable results the beginnings of a more critical inquiry into the records of the ancient Hebrew religion. Indeed, the author of the "Prolegomena" himself clearly foresaw the influence which his book was destined to exert on Hebrew

---

[1] In a letter given in Körte's "Leben und Studien F. A Wolf's." i., p. 307.

[2] Scientific pursuits are distinguished from others, not by the material, but by the method of knowledge. The mere collection of data, however multiplied in detail, however abstruse the subjects to which they may refer, does not of itself deserve the name of science. The term properly applies only when phenomena are placed in causal relation, and the laws which govern their development are traced. Measured by this standard, every attempt to explain the growth of human thought and institutions, and to elucidate the laws which have acted in the process of their evolution, has a just claim to be classed under the head of scientific inquiry.

studies. In a letter, from which we have already quoted above, he says: "The demonstration that the Pentateuch is made up of unequal portions, that these are the products of different centuries, and that they were put together shortly after the time of Solomon, may, ere long, be confidently expected. I should myself be willing to undertake such an argument without fear, for nowhere do we find any ancient witness to guarantee the authorship of the Pentateuch to Moses himself." [1]

The prediction embodied in these words soon came true. A host of competent scholars took up the study of the Hebrew Bible, and, profiting by Wolf's example and suggestions, applied to its elucidation the same careful methods, the same scrupulous honesty of interpretation, that had proved so successful in the realm of classical philology. Theologians by profession, they set aside their predilections, and placed the ascertainment of the truth above all other interests. They believed in the indestructible vitality of religion, and were willing to admit the full light of criticism upon the scriptural page, confident that any loss would be temporary only, the gain permanent. In the course of their researches they arrived, among others, at the following important conclusions:

That the editor of the Pentateuch had admitted into his volume several accounts touching the main facts of early Hebrew history; that these accounts are often mutually at variance; that minute analysis and careful comparison alone can lead to an approximately true estimate of their comparative value; and, lastly, that the transmission of historical information had in no wise been the object of the Hebrew writers. The history of their people served, it is true, to illustrate certain of their doctrines concerning the divine government of the world, and especially the peculiar relations of the Deity to the chosen race; but it was employed much in the sense of a moral tale, being designed, not to convey facts, but to enforce lessons. Had the acceptance of any particular scheme of Hebrew history been deemed essential to the integrity of religious belief, the Bible, they argued, would certainly not have included discrepant accounts of that history in its pages. In the light of this new

[1] Letter in Körte's "Leben und Studien F. A. Wolf's," i., p. 309.

insight, it seemed advisable to draw a distinction between the biblical narrative proper and the doctrines which it was designed to illustrate. The latter belong to the province of faith, and their treatment may be left to the expounders of faith. The former is a department of general history, and in dealing with it we are at liberty to apply the same canons of criticism that obtain in every other department, without fearing to trespass upon sacred ground. It is our purpose in the following pages to present some of the more interesting results that have been reached in the study of the Pentateuch, so far as they illustrate the evolution of religious ideas among the Hebrews. We shall begin by summarizing a few instances of discrepant testimony to introduce our subject, and, in particular, to show how little the ordinary purposes of history have been considered in the composition of the biblical writings; how little the bare transmission of facts was an object with the sacred authors.[1]

The Scriptures open with two divergent accounts of the creation. In Genesis i., the work of creation proceeds in two grand movements, including the formation of inanimate and animate Nature respectively.[2] On the first day a diffused light is spread out over chaos. Then are made the firmament, the dry earth, the green herbs, and fruit-bearing trees; on the fourth day the great luminaries are called into being; on the fifth, the fishes and birds of the air; on the sixth, the beasts of the field; and, lastly, crowning all, man, his Maker's masterpiece. The human species enters at once upon its existence *as a pair*. "Male and female did he create them." In the second chapter the same methodical arrangement, the same deliberate progress from the lower to the higher forms of being, is not observed. Man, his interests and responsibilities, stand in the foreground of the picture. The trees of the field are not made until after Adam; and, subsequently to them, the cattle and beasts. Moreover, man is a solitary being. A comparison between his lonely condition and the dual existence of the remainder of the animal

---

[1] Many of the following examples are familiarly known. A few, however, are drawn from recent investigations. Compare, especially, Kuenen, "The Religion of Israel."

[2] Tuch's "Genesis," p. 3, second edition, Halle, 1871.

APPENDIX. 187

world leads the Deity to determine upon the creation of woman. A profound slumber then falls upon Adam, a rib is taken from his side, and from it Eve is fashioned.[1] We may observe that the name Jehovah, as appertaining to the Deity, is employed in the second chapter, while it is scrupulously avoided in the first. The recognition of this distinction has led to further discoveries of far-reaching importance, but too complicated in their nature to be here detailed. The conflicting statements of the two accounts, which we have just indicated, have induced scholars to regard them as the work of different writers. In Genesis iv. we learn that in the days of Enoch, Adam's grandson, men began to call on the name of Jehovah; in Exodus vi., on the contrary, that the name Jehovah was first revealed to Moses, being unknown even to the patriarchs.

Gen. xvi., Hagar is driven from her home by the jealousy of her mistress; escapes into the desert; beholds a vision of God at a well in a wilderness. Gen. xxi., the flight of Hagar is related a second time. The general scheme of the narrative is the same as above; but there are important divergencies of detail. As narrated in chapter xvi., the escape took place immediately before the birth of Ishmael. Fifteen years elapsed,[2] and Ishmael, now approaching the years of maturity, is once more driven forth from the house of Abraham. But, to our surprise, in chapter xxi. the lad is described as a mere infant; he is carried on his mother's shoulders, and laid away, like a helpless babe, under some bushes by the wayside. It appears that we have before us two accounts touching the same event, agreeing in the main incidents of the escape, but showing a disagreement of fifteen years as to the date of its occurrence. The narratives are distinguished as above by the employment of dif-

---

[1] For an account of the close analogy between the biblical narration and the Persian story of Meshja and Meshjane, their temptation and fall, *vide* ibid. p. 40. It is of special importance to note that reference to the account of Genesis ii. is made only in the later literature of the Hebrews, ibid., p. 42.

[2] Gen. xvii. 25. In quoting from the Old Testament, we follow the order of the Hebrew text.

ferent names of the Deity: Jehovah in the one instance, Elohim in the other.

Gen. xxxii., Jacob at the fords of Jabbok, after wrestling during the night with a divine being, receives the name of Israel. Gen. xxxv., without reference to the previous account, the name Israel is conferred upon Jacob at a different place and under different circumstances.

Gen. xlix., the dispersion of the Levites among the tribes is characterized as a punishment and a curse. They are to be forever homeless and fugitive. Deuteronomy xxxiii. and elsewhere, it is described as a blessing. The Levites have been scattered as good seed over the land. They are apostles, commissioned to propagate Jehovah's law.

Passing on to the second book of the Pentateuch, we pause before the account of the Revelation on Mount Sinai, beyond a doubt the most important event of Israel's ancient history. Exodus xxiv. 2, Moses alone is to approach the divine presence. Exod. xix. 24, Aaron is to accompany him. Exod. xxiv. 13, Aaron is to remain below and Joshua is to go in his stead. Again, Exod. xxxiii. 20, instant death will overtake him who beholds God. Exod. xxiv. 9-11, Moses, Aaron, two of his sons, and seventy elders of Israel "ascended, and they saw the God of Israel. . . . Also, they saw God, and did eat and drink." Once more, Exod. xxiv. 4-7, Moses himself writes down the words of revelation in a book of covenant. Exod. xxiv. 12, not Moses but God writes them; and, elsewhere, "Two tables of stone inscribed by the finger of God."

Exod. xx. enjoins the observance of the sabbath-day as a memorial of the repose of the Maker of heaven and earth on the sabbath of creation. Deut. v., the fourth commandment is enjoined because of the redemption of Israel from Egyptian bondage. Exod. xxxiv., a new version of the decalogue, differing in most respects from the one commonly received, is promulgated.[1] The first commandment is to worship no strange god; the second, to make no graven images; the third, to observe the feast

[1] Compare De Wette's "Einleitung in das alte Testament" (Schrader's edition), p. 286, note 53.

APPENDIX.

of unleavened bread; the fourth, to deliver the first-born unto Jehovah; the fifth, to observe the sabbath, etc.

In Exod. xx. we read that the guilt of the fathers will be avenged upon the children down even to the third and fourth generation; in Deut. xxiv., the children shall not die for their fathers. Every one for his own sin shall die.

In Deut. xxv. the marrying of a deceased brother's wife is under certain conditions enjoined as a duty. In Levit. xviii. it is unconditionally prohibited as a crime.

Exod. xxxiii., Moses removes the tabernacle beyond the camp. Num. ii., the tabernacle rests in the very heart of the camp, with all the tribes of Israel grouped round about it, according to their standards and divisions.

Num. xvi., the sons of Korah, the leader of the great Levitical sedition, perish with their father. Num. xxvi., the sons of Korah do not perish.[1]

Of the forty years which the Israelites are said to have dwelt in the desert, not more than two are covered by the events of the narrative. The remainder are wrapped in dense obscurity. There is, however, a significant fact which deserves mention in this connection. The death of Aaron marks, as it were, the close of Israel's journey. Now, while in Num. xxxiii. the death of the high-priest is described as occurring in the fortieth year, in Deut. x. it is actually referred to the second year of the Exodus.[2]

A brief digression beyond the borders of the Pentateuch will

---

[1] Num. xxvi. 11. Indeed, had the sons of Korah and every human being related to him perished, as Num. xvi. avers, how could we account for the fact that Korah's descendants filled high offices in the Temple at Jerusalem later on? The celebrated singer, Heman, himself was a lineal descendant of Korah. To the descendants of Korah also are ascribed the following Psalms: Ps. xlii., xliv.–xlix., lxxxiv., lxxxv., lxxxvii., lxxxviii.

[2] In connection with this subject it is of interest to compare Goethe's argument in the "Westöstlicher Divan" on the duration of the desert journey. Here, as in so many other instances, the intuitive perception of the great poet anticipated the tardy results of subsequent investigation.

show that the conflict of testimony which we have thus far noticed, affecting as it does some of the leading events of ancient Hebrew history, does not diminish as we proceed in the narrative. In 1 Samuel vii. it is said that the Philistines ceased to harass the land of Israel all the days of Samuel. Immediately thereupon we read of new Philistine incursions more direful than ever in their consequences.[1] The popular proverb, "Is Saul among the prophets?" is variously explained, 1 Sam. x. and xix. Two discrepant accounts are given of Saul's rejection from the kingdom, 1 Sam. xiii. and xv.; of David's introduction to Saul, 1 Sam. xvi. and xvii. The charming story of David's encounter with the giant Goliath told in 1 Sam. xvii. is contradicted in 2 Sam. xxi. 19, where, not David, but some person otherwise unknown to fame, is reported to have slain the giant Goliath, and also the time, place, and attendant circumstances, are differently related.[2]

It thus appears that the compiler of the Pentateuch has admitted a variety of views, not only on the ancient history of his people, but also on the general subject of religion and morals, into his work; and that the discordant opinions of diverse authors and of diverse stages of human progress are reflected in its pages. It is the monument of a grand religious movement extending over many centuries of gradual development. It is the image of a nation's struggles and growth. As contained in the books of the Pentateuch, the Mosaic religion is a religious mosaic.

In the foregoing sketch we have observed how deep a mist of uncertainty hangs over the earliest period, the golden age of the history of the Hebrews. All is in a state of flux, and what appeared compact and coherent at a distance yields to our touch upon closer contact. To gain *terra firma*, let us turn to the period which immediately succeeded the settlement of the Israelites in Palestine; a period in which the outline of historical events begins to assume a more definite and tangible shape.

[1] Compare 1 Sam. vii. 13, and 1 Sam. xiii. 19.
[2] In 1 Chron. xx. 5, we read, "the brother of Goliath." The purpose of the change is clear, and accords well with the apologetical tendencies of the author of Chronicles. *Vide* De Wette, "Einleitung," etc., p. 370. Geiger, "Urschrift."

APPENDIX. 191

It was a dismal and sorrowful age. The bonds of social order were loosened; the current conceptions of the Deity and the rites of his worship were gross and often degrading. Mutual jealousies kindled the firebrand of war among the contending clans. Almost the whole tribe of Benjamin was extirpated. Abimelech slew seventy princes upon one stone. Lust and treachery ran riot. A wilder deed has never been chronicled in the annals of mankind than that related in chapter xix. of Judges, nor ever has a terrible deed been more terribly avenged. Now, looking backward, we ask, Is it to be believed that in the fourteenth century B. C. not only the leader of Israel, but also their elders, their priests, nay, large numbers of the very populace, shared in the most exalted, the most spiritual conceptions of God, and nourished the most refined sentiments in regard to human relationships, while immediately thereupon, and centuries thereafter, violence and bloodshed, and idolatry, do not cease from the records? It has been argued, indeed, that the worship of idols was but a *relapse* from the purity of a preceding age; and that, though the tradition of the Mosaic time may have been lost in the succeeding period among the people at large, it was still preserved in the circle of a select few, the judges, King David, and others. These, it is believed, continued to remain faithful disciples of the great lawgiver. But these very men, the judges—King David himself—all fall immeasurably below the standard that is set up in the Pentateuch. If they were esteemed the true representatives of the national religion in their day, if the very points in which they transgressed the provisions of the Mosaic code are distinguished by the approval of God and man, we are forced to conclude that that standard—by which they stand condemned—did not yet exist; that, in the days of David, the laws of Moses, as we now have them, were as yet unwritten and unknown. Let us illustrate this important point by a few examples taken from the records. Gideon no sooner returns from victory than he makes a golden idol and sets it up for worship. Jephthah slays his daughter as an offering of thanksgiving to Jehovah. In the Pentateuch the adoration of images is branded as the gravest of offences. David keeps household gods in his own home (Sam. xix). In the Pentateuch, on its opening page, God is proclaimed as a pure spirit, maker of heaven and earth. In the eyes of David (1 Sam, xxvi. 19), the sway of Jehovah does not extend beyond the borders of Palestine.[1] In the Pentateuch the ark of the covenant is described as the treasury of all that is brightest and best in the worship of the one God. None but the consecrated priest dare approach it, and even he only under circumstances calculated to inspire peculiar veneration and awe. In 2 Sam. vi., David abandons the ark to the keeping of a heathen Philistine. In an early age of culture, when fear and terror in the presence of superior force entered largely into the religious conceptions of the Hebrews, the taking of the census was deemed an act of grave transgression. It appeared a vaunting of one's strength ; it seemed to indicate a defiant attitude toward the loftier power of the Deity, which he would certainly visit with condign punishment. At a later period the priesthood found it in their interest to override these scruples, and the taking of the census became an affair of habitual occurrence. In the last chapter of Samuel the more primitive view still predominated. Seventy thousand Israelites are miserably slain to atone for King David's presumption in commanding a census of the people. In the fourth book of Moses, on the other hand, the numbering of the people not only proceeds without the slightest evil resulting therefrom, but at the express command of God himself.

In the book of Deuteronomy the service of Jehovah is said to consist mainly in the practice of righteousness, in works of kindness toward our fellows, in sincere and holy love toward the Deity, who is represented as the merciful father of all his human children. Second Sam. xxi., a famine comes upon the land of Israel. The anger of Jehovah is kindled against the people. To appease him, David offers sacrifice—human sacrifice. The seven sons of Saul are slain, and their bodies kept exposed on the hill, " in sight of Jehovah," and the horrid offering *is accepted*, and the divine wrath is thereby pacified.[2] Truly, in the age of

[1] Banishment being described as a transfer of allegiance to strange gods.

[2] It is important to note that the seven sons of Saul were sacrificed

APPENDIX. 193

David, the Hebrews were far, far removed from the high state of culture in which the ideal conception of religion that pervades Deuteronomy became possible. And long after, when centuries had gone by and the kingdom of Judah was already approaching its dissolution, the direful practices of David's reign still survived, and the root of idolatry had not been plucked from the heart of the people. Still do we hear of human sacrifice perpetrated in the midst of Jerusalem, and steeds and chariots dedicated to the sun-god, and images of the Phallus, and all the abominations of sensual worship, filled the very Temple of Jehovah.

But in the meantime a new force had entered the current of Hebrew history. The conviction that one God, and he an all-just, almighty being, ruled the destinies of Israel, began to take root. In the eighth century B. C. authentic records prove that monotheism, as a form of religious belief, obtained, at least among the more illustrious members of the prophetic order. We have elsewhere attempted to trace the causes which led to the rise of monotheism at this particular epoch, and can do no more than briefly allude to them here.

When the mountaineers of Southern Palestine, after centuries of protracted struggles, had secured the safe possession of individual homes, the endearments of domestic life were invested with a sanctity in their eyes never before known. The attachment of the Hebrew toward his offspring was intensified; his devotion to the wife of his bosom became purer and more enduring. Now, the prevailing forms of Semitic religion outraged these feelings at every point. The gods of the surrounding nations were gods of pleasure and of pain; and in their worship the stern practices of fanatic asceticism alternated with the wildest orgies of sensual enjoyment. The worship of Baal Moloch demanded the sacrifice of children; that of the lasciv-

---

in the beginning of the barley-harvest. This circumstance seems to throw light on the primitive mode of celebrating the Passover. That the rite of human sacrifice was originally connected with this festival is generally acknowledged. *Vide*, e. g., Exod. xiii., 2. By such offerings it was intended, no doubt, to secure the favor of the god during the continuance of the harvest.

ious Baaltis insulted the modesty of woman. The nobler spirits among the Hebrews rebelled against both these demands. And, as the latter were put forth in the name of the dominant religion, the inevitable conclusion followed that that religion itself must be radically wrong. The spirit of opposition thus awakened was aroused into powerful activity when, in the days of Ahab, the queen, supported by an influential priesthood, determined to introduce the forms of Phœnician religion in Israel by measures of force. The royal edicts were resisted, but for a while the rule of the stronger prevailed. The leaders of the opposition were compelled to flee, and, avoiding the habitations of men, to take refuge in wild and solitary places. Thus the rupture was widened into schism, and persecution inflamed the zeal and kindled the energies of that new order of men of whom Elijah is the well-known type.

Through their agency the emotional nature of the Semitic race now found expression in a form of religious worship loftier by far than any that had ever arisen among men. If Baal was the embodiment of Semitic asceticism and Baaltis the type of sensual orgiastic passion, the national God of Israel now became the type of a nobler emotion, the guardian of domestic purity, the source of sanctity, the ideal Father. It is indeed the image of a just patriarch that fills the mind and wings the fancy of the eldest prophets, when they describe the nature of Jehovah, their God. Jehovah is the husband of the people. Israel shall be his true and loyal spouse. The children of Israel are his children. Unchastity and irreligion are synonymous terms. And thus, if we err not, the peculiar feature of Hebrew character, their faithful attachment to kith and kin, the strength and purity of their domestic affections, serves to explain the peculiar character, the origin and development of the Hebrew religion. And because the essential elements of the new religion were moral elements it could not tolerate the Nature-worship of the heathens; and the way was prepared for the gradual ascendency of the purely spiritual in religion, which after ages of gradual progress constituted the last, the lasting triumph of prophecy.

After ages of development! For we are not to suppose that, in the centuries succeeding Hosea, the doctrines of the prophetic schools had become in any sense the property of the people at large. "The powers that be" were arrayed against them, and the annals of the kings are replete with evidence of their sufferings. It was in the late reign of Josiah that they at last received not only the countenance of the reigning monarch, but also a decisive influence upon the direction of affairs. In that reign a scroll was found in the temple imbued with the doctrine of the unity of God, and breathing the vigorous spirit of the prophets. In it was emphasized the heart's religion in preference to the empty ceremonial of priestly worship. The allegiance of the people was directed toward the God who had elected them from among the nations of the earth, and dire disaster was predicted in case of disobedience. When brought to the king and read in his presence, he was powerfully affected, and determined, if possible, to stem the tide of impending ruin by such salutary measures of reform as the injunctions of the newly-found Scripture seemed most urgently to call for. The concurrence of many critics has identified this scroll, written and published at or about the time when the youthful Josiah succeeded to the throne of his ancestors, with Deuteronomy, the fifth of the books of Moses. It differs materially from the more recent writings of the Pentateuch. The family of Aaron are not yet exclusively endowed with the priesthood. The priests are all Levites, the Levites all priests. There are, moreover, other vital differences, into which the limits of this article do not permit us to enter.[1] The date of the composition of Deuteronomy is thus referred to the closing decades of the seventh century B. C.[2]

The princes who succeeded Josiah fell back into the old course, and quite undid the work which had begun with such fair promise. Indeed, little permanent good was to be hoped for in so disordered a condition of political affairs, and from the degenerate rulers who then swayed the helm of state. The for-

[1] E. g., the rebellion of Korah is unknown to the author of Deuteronomy.

[2] The language of Deuteronomy attests its late origin. Sixty-six phrases of Deuteronomy recur in the writings of Jeremiah. *Vide* Zunz, *Zeitschrift der Deutschen Morgenländischen Gesellschaft*, xxviii., p. 670.

tunes of the kingdom of Judah were swiftly declining, and, not fully a quarter of a century after the pious Josiah had breathed his last, Nebuchadnezzar burned the Temple of Jerusalem, and carried its inhabitants captive to Babylon.

Heretofore, with but a brief, brilliant interlude, idolatry had been the court religion of Judah. Early training, long usage, the example of revered ancestors, had endeared its forms and symbols to the affections of the people. Resistance to the innovating prophets was natural; men being then, as ever, loath to abandon the sacred usages which had come down to them from the distant generations of the past. But, in the long years of the captivity, a profound change came over the spirit of the Hebrew people; "by Babel's streams they sat and wept;" by Babel's streams they recalled the memories of their native land, that land which they had lost. It was then that the voices of Jehovah's messengers, which had so earnestly warned them of the approaching doom, recurred to their startled recollection. They remembered the message; they beheld its fulfillment; the testimony of the prophets had been confirmed by events; the one God to whom they testified had revealed his omnipotence in history; and with ready assent the exiles promised allegiance to his commandments in the future. The love of country, the dread of further chastisement, the dear hope of restoration, combined to win them to the purer worship of their God, and, in the crucible of Babylon, the national religion was purged of the last dregs of heathendom.

With the permission of Cyrus, the Jews returned to Palestine and the Temple at Jerusalem was rebuilt. The question now arose in what forms the ceremonial of the new sanctuary should be conducted. The time-honored festivals, the solemn and joyful convocations, the sacrifices and purifications of the olden time, were all more or less infected with the taint of paganism. Prophecy would have none of them—prophecy, free child of genius, contemned sacrifice, denounced the priesthood, even the temple and its ritual;[1] proclaimed humbleness and loving-kindness as the true service in which Jehovah takes delight. There was formalism on the one hand, idealism on the other. As is

---

[1] Jeremiah vii. 4; Isaiah lxvi. 1; Micah vi. 6.

usual in such cases, when the time had arrived for turning theory into practice, it was found necessary to effect a compromise. As Christianity in later days adopted the yule-tree into its system, and lit the lamps of the heathen festival of the 25th of December in honor of the nativity of its founder, so the leaders of the Jews, in the fifth century before our era, adopted the feasts and usages of an ancient Nature-worship, breathed into them a new spirit, informed them with a loftier meaning, and made them tokens, symbols of the eternal God. The old foes were thus reconciled; priesthood and prophecy joined hands, and were thenceforth united. As an offspring of this union, we behold a new code of laws and prescriptions, whose marked and inharmonious features at once betray the dual nature of its progenitors. "A rough preliminary draft, as it were," of this code, is preserved in the book of Ezekiel, composed probably about the middle of the fifth century. In its finished and final shape, it forms the bulk of a still later work—of Leviticus, namely the third of the books of the Pentateuch: of all the discoveries of criticism none more noteworthy, none we are permitted to consider more assured. What lends additional certainty to the result is the circumstance that it was reached independently by two of the most esteemed scholars of our day, the one a Professor of Theology in the University of Leyden,[1] the other a veteran of thought, whose brow is wreathed by the ripe honors of more than fourscore years.[2] Let us briefly advert to the line of argument by which this astonishing conclusion was reached:

The author of the book of Ezekiel was a priest, and one confessedly loyal to the sanctuary of Jerusalem. Now, had the laws of the Levitical code, which minutely describe the ritual of that sanctuary, existed, or been regarded as authoritative in his day, he could not, would not have disregarded, much less contradicted, their provisions. He does this, and, be it remarked, in points of capital importance. In chapter xlv. of Ezekiel are mentioned the great festivals, with the sacrifices appropriate to each; but the feast of Pentecost, commanded in Leviticus, is entirely omitted; also that of the eighth day of tabernacles. The second of the daily burnt-offerings, upon which the legis-

[1] Prof. A. Kuenen.   [2] The venerable Dr. Zunz, of Berlin.

lator of the fourth book of Moses dwells with such marked emphasis, is not commanded. The order of sacrifices appointed in Ezekiel is at variance with that in the more recent code. Ezekiel nowhere mentions the ark of the covenant. According to him, the new year begins on the tenth of the seventh month, while the festival of the trumpets, ordained in Leviticus for the first of that month (the present new year of the Jews), is nowhere referred to. We are not to suppose, however, that the festivals, the ark, etc., did not yet exist in the time of Ezekiel. They existed, no doubt, but were still too intimately associated with pagan customs and superstitions to receive or merit the countenance of a prophetic writer. In Leviticus the process of assimilation above described had reached its climax. The new meaning had been successfully engrafted upon the rites and symbols of the olden time; and they were thenceforth freely employed. The legislation of the Levitical code exhibits the familiar features which in every instance mark the ascendency or consolidation of the hierarchical order. The lines of gradation and distinction between the members of the order among themselves are precisely drawn and strictly adhered to. The prerogatives of the whole order as against the people are fenced about with stringent laws. The revenues of the order are largely increased. In the older code of Deuteronomy, the annual tithes were set apart for a festival occasion, and given over to the enjoyment of the people. In the new code, the hierarchy claims the tithes for its own use. New taxes are invented. The best portions of the sacrificial animal are reserved for the banquets of the Temple. The first-born of men and cattle belong to the priesthood, and must be ransomed by the payment of a sum of money. In no period prior to the fifth century B. C. was the hierarchy powerful enough to design such laws. At that time, however, when in the absence of a temporal sovereign they, with the high-priest at their head, were the acknowledged rulers of the state, they were both prepared to conceive and able to carry them into effect. The language of Leviticus contributes not a little to betray its late origin.[1] The

[1] To mention only a single instance, ha Shem (meaning the name, i. e. the ineffable name of God) was not employed until a very late

authorship of Moses attributed to the Levitical code is symbolical. *The name of Moses is utterly unknown to the elder prophets.* In all their manifold writings it does not occur a single time, though they make frequent reference to the past. There can now be little doubt that the composition of the bulk of Leviticus, and of considerable portions of the books of Numbers, Exodus, and even parts of Genesis, belongs to the epoch of the second Temple, and that the date of these writings may be approximately fixed at about one thousand years after the time of Moses. As to the story of Israel's desert wanderings, it rests upon ancient traditions whose character it is not our present business to investigate. It was successively worked up in various schools of priests and prophets, and this accounts for the host of discrepancies it contains, some of which have been noticed in the beginning of this essay. It was finally amplified by the inventive genius of the second-Temple priesthood, who succeeded in heightening the sanctity of their own institutions by tracing them back to a revered, heroic person, who had lived in the dim days of remote antiquity.

In the preceding pages we have indicated the more important phases of that conflict which ended in the establishment of monotheism, a conflict whose traces, though sometimes barely legible, are still preserved in our records. We saw in the first instance that the Mosaic age is shrouded in uncertainty. We pointed out that pure monotheism was unknown in the time of the early kings. We briefly referred to the rise of monotheism. Finally, we endeavored to show how the prophetic idea had been successively expressed in various codes, each corresponding to a certain stage in the great process of evolution. From what we have said, it follows that the prophetic ideal of religion is the root and core of all that is valuable in the Hebrew Bible. The laws, rites, and observances, in which it found a temporary and changeful expression, may lose their vitality ; it will always continue to exert its high influence. It was not the work of one man, nor of a single age, but was reached in the long course of

period in the history of the Jews, when the fear of taking the name of the Lord in vain induced men to avoid, if possible, mentioning it at all. We find ha Shem in the above sense in Lev. xxiv. 11.

generations on generations, evolved amid error and vice, slowly, and against all the odds of time. It has been said that the Bible is opposed to the theory of evolution. The Bible itself is a prominent example of evolution in history. It is not homogeneous in all its parts. There are portions filled with tales of human error and fallibility. These are the incipient stages of an early age—the dark and dread beginnings. There are others thrilling with noblest emotion, freighted with eternal truths, breathing celestial music. These are the triumph and the fruition of a later day. It is thus by discriminating between what is essentially excellent and what is comparatively valueless that we shall best reconcile the discordant claims of reason and of faith. The Bible was never designed to convey scientific information, nor was it intended to serve as a text-book of history. In its ethical teachings lies its true significance. On them it may fairly rest its claims to the immortal reverence of mankind.

There was a time in the olden days of Greece when it was demanded that the poems of Homer should be removed from the schools, lest the minds of the young might be poisoned by the weeds of superstitious belief. Plato, the poet-philosopher, it was who urged this demand. That time is past. The tales of the gods and heroes have long since ceased to entice our credulity. The story of Achilles's wrath and the wanderings of the sage Ulysses are not believed as history, but the beauty and freshness and the golden poetry of the Homeric epic have a reality all their own, and are a delight and a glory now, as they have ever been before. The Bible also is a classical book. It is the classical book of noble ethical sentiment. In it the mortal fear, the overflowing hope, the quivering longings of the human soul toward the better and the best, have found their first, their freshest, their fittest utterance. In this respect it can never be superseded.

To Greek philosophy we owe the evolution of the logical categories; to Hebrew prophecy, the pure canon of moral principle and action. That this result was the outcome of a long process of suffering and struggle cannot diminish its value in our estimation. When we compare the degrading offices of the Hebrew religion in the days of the judges with the lofty aspirations of the second Isaiah, when we remember the utter abyss of moral abasement from which the nobler spirits of the Hebrews rose to the free heights of prophecy, our confidence in the divine possibilities of the human soul is reinvigorated, our emulation is kindled, and from the great things already accomplished we gather the cheering promise of the greater things that are yet to come. It is in this moral incentive that the practical value of the evolutionary theory chiefly lies.[1]

[1] Most aptly has this thought been expressed in the lines with which Goethe welcomed the appearance of F. A. Wolf's "Prolegomena:"

"Erst die Gesundheit des Mannes, der, endlich vom Namen Homeros
Kühn uns befreiend, uns auch führt in die vollere Bahn.
Denn wer wagte mit Göttern den Kampf? und wer mit dem Einen?—
Doch Homeride zu seyn, auch nur als letzter, ist schön."
The Elegy of Hermann und Dorothea.

II.

REFORMED JUDAISM.

THE Jews are justly called a peculiar people. During the past three thousand years they have lived apart from their fellow-men, in a state of voluntary or enforced isolation. The laws of the Pentateuch directed them to avoid contact with heathens. Christianity in turn shunned and execrated them. Proud and sensitive by nature, subjected to every species of humiliation and contempt, they retired upon themselves, and continued to be what the seer from Aram had described them in the olden time, "A people that dwells in solitude."[1] It followed that, in the progress of time, idiosyncrasies of character were developed, and habits of thinking and feeling grew up amongst them, which could not but contribute to alienate them still more from the surrounding world. They felt that they were not understood. They were too shy to open their confidence to their oppressors. They remained an enigma. At wide intervals books appeared purporting to give an account of the Jews and their sacred customs. But these attempts were, in the main, dictated by no just or generous motive. Their authors, narrow bigots or renegades from Judaism, ransacked the vast literature of the Hebrew people for such scattered fragments as might be used to their discredit, and exhibited these as samples of Jewish manners and Jewish religion. The image thus presented, it is needless to say, was extremely untrustworthy. And yet the writings of these partial judges have remained almost the only sources from which even many modern writers are accustomed to draw their information. The historian is yet to come who will dispel the dense mists of prejudice that have gathered about Jewish history, and reveal the inward life of this

[1] Numbers xxiii. 9.

wonderful people, whose perennial freshness has been preserved through so many centuries of the most severe trials and persecution. In one respect, indeed, let us hasten to add, the popular judgment concerning the Jews has never been deceived. The intense conservatism in religion for which they have become proverbial is fully confirmed by facts. There exists no other race of men that has approved its fidelity to religious conviction for an equal period, under equal difficulties, and amid equal temptations. Antiochus, Titus, Firuz, Reccared, Edward I. of England, Philip Augustus of France, Ferdinand of Spain, exhausted the resources of tyranny in vain to shake their constancy. Their power of resistance rose with the occasion that called it forth; and their fervid loyalty to the faith transmitted to them by the fathers never appeared to greater advantage than when it cost them their peace, their happiness, and their life to maintain it. Since the close of the last century, however, a great change has apparently come over the Jewish people. Not only have they abandoned their former attitude of reserve and mingled freely with their fellow-citizens of whatever creed, not only have they taken a leading part in the great political revolutions that swept over Europe, but the passion for change, so characteristic of the age in which we live, has extended even to their time-honored religion; and a movement aiming at nothing less than the complete reformation of Judaism has arisen, and rapidly acquired the largest dimensions. The very fact that such a movement should exist among such a people is rightly interpreted as a sign of the times deserving of careful and candid consideration; and great interest has accordingly been manifested of late on the subject of Jewish Reform. In a series of articles we shall undertake to give a brief sketch of the origin and bearings of the movement. But before addressing ourselves to this task it will be necessary to review a few of the main causes that have enabled the Jews to perdure in history, and to consider the motives that impelled them to resist change so long, if we would properly appreciate the process of transformation that is even now taking place among them. Among the efficient forces that conduced to the preservation of the Jewish people we rank highest:

THE PURITY OF THEIR DOMESTIC RELATIONS.

The sacredness of the family tie is the condition both of the physical soundness and the moral vigor of nations. The family is the miniature commonwealth, upon whose integrity the safety of the larger commonwealth depends. It is the seedplot of all morality. In the child's intercourse with its parents the sentiment of reverence is instilled—the essence of all piety, all idealism; also the habit of obedience to rightful authority, which forms so invaluable a feature in the character of the loyal citizen. In the companionship of brothers deference to the rights of equals is practically inculcated, without which no community could exist. The relations between brother and sister give birth to the sentiment of chivalry,—regard for the rights of the weaker,—and this forms the basis of magnanimity, and every generous and tender quality that graces humanity. Reverence for superiors, respect for equals, regard for inferiors,—these form the supreme trinity of the virtues. Whatever is great and good in the institutions and usages of mankind is an application of sentiments that have drawn their first nourishment from the soil of the family. The family is the school of duties. But it has this distinguishing excellency, that among those who are linked together by the strong ties of affection duty is founded on love. On this account it becomes typical of the perfect morality in all the relations of life, and we express the noblest longings of the human heart when we speak of a time to come in which all mankind will be united "as one family." Now the preëminence of the Jews in point of domestic purity will hardly be disputed. "In this respect they stand out like a bold promontory in the history of the past, singular and unapproached," said the philosopher Trendelenburg.[1] According to the provisions of the Mosaic Code, the crime of adultery is punished with death. The most minute directions are given touching the dress of the priests and the common people, in order to check the pruriency of fancy. The scale of forbidden marriages is widely extended

[1] Vide the essay on the Origin of Monotheism in Jahrbuch des Vereins für Wissenschaftliche Pädagogik, Vol. IX. 1877, by the author of this article.

with the same end in view. Almost the entire tribe of Benjamin is extirpated to atone for an outrage upon feminine virtue committed within its borders. The undutiful son is stoned to death in the presence of the whole people. That husband and wife shall become "as one flesh," is a conception which we find only among the Jews. Among them the picture of the true housewife which is unrolled to us in Proverbs had its original,— the picture of her who unites all womanly grace and gentleness, in whose environment dwell comfort and beauty, "whose husband and sons rise up to praise her." The marriage tie was held so sacred that it was freely used by the prophets to describe the relations between the Deity and the chosen people. Jehovah is called the husband of the people. Israel shall be his true and loyal spouse. The children of Israel are his children. The worship of false gods was designated by the Hebrew word that signifies conjugal infidelity. This feature of Jewish life remained equally prominent in later times. In the age of the Talmud marriage was called Hillula,—a song of praise! The most holy day of the year, the tenth of the seventh month, a day of fasting and the atonement of sins, was deemed a proper occasion to collect the young people for the purpose of choosing husbands and wives. On that day the maidens of Jerusalem, arrayed in pure white, went out into the vineyards that covered the slopes of the neighboring hills, dancing as they went, and singing as the bands of youth came up to meet them from the valleys. "Youth, raise now thine eyes," sang the beautiful among them, "and regard her whom thou choosest." Look not to beauty," sang the well-born, "but rather to ancient lineage and high descent." Lastly, those who were neither beautiful nor well born took up the strain, and thus they sang: "Treacherous is grace, and beauty deceitful; the woman that fears God alone shall be praised." The appropriateness of such proceedings on the Atonement day was justified by the remark that marriage is itself an act of spiritual purification. The high value attached to the institution of the family is further illustrated by many tender legends of the Talmud which we cannot here stop to recount. A separate gate, it is said, was reserved in Solomon's Temple for the use of bridegrooms, before which they received the felicitations of the assembled people. The marriage celebration was essentially a festival of religion. Seven days it lasted. The Talmudic law, usually so unbending in its exactions, relaxed its austerity in favor of these auspicious occasions, and recommended to all to rejoice with the joyful. On the Sabbath of the marriage-week, the young husband was received with peculiar honors in the synagogue, and the liturgy of the mediæval Jews is crowded with hymns composed in honor of these solemn receptions. If a whole congregation thus united to magnify and sanctify the erection of a new home, the continued preservation of its sanctity might safely be left to the jealous watchfulness of its inmates. Cases of sensual excess or of unfilial conduct have been extremely infrequent among the Jews, down to modern times. However mean the outward appearance of their homes might be, the moral atmosphere that pervaded them was rarely contaminated. If the question be asked, how it came about that so feeble a people could resist the malevolence of its foes ; that a nation, deprived of any visible rallying-point, with no political or religious centre to cement their union, had not long since been wiped out from the earth's surface, we answer that the *hearth* was their rallying-point and the centre of their union. There the scattered atoms gained consistency sufficient to withstand the pressure of the world. Thither they could come to recreate their torn and lacerated spirits. There was the well-spring of their power.

THE SCHOOLS.

If the Jewish people were preserved in moral vigor by the influence of their domestic life, the care they bestowed on the education of the young kept them intellectually fresh. Schools were erected in every town and country district. It was forbidden a Jew to reside in cities where no provision had been made for the instruction of children. Teachers were called the guardians of cities. The destruction of Jerusalem was attributed to the fact that the schools had been suffered to fall into neglect. Synagogues were often used for purposes of primary instruction. "A sage is greater than a prophet," said the proverb. To increase in knowledge, at least in a certain kind of knowledge, was a part of the Jew's religion. According to the theory of the Rabbies the revelation of God to man is fully embodied in the books of the Old Testament, especially in the books of the Pentateuch, commonly called the Tora,—the Law. They contain, either by direct statement or by implication, whatever it is necessary for men to know. They anticipate all future legislation. Though apparently scanty in substance, they are replete with suggestions of profound and inexhaustible wisdom. To penetrate the hidden meanings of "the Law" became, on this account, the primary obligation of the devout; and ignorance was not only despised on its own account, but was, in addition, branded as a sign of deficient piety. The ordinances of the Jewish sages are all ostensibly deduced from the words of the Sacred Law. Without such sanction no enactment of any later lawgiver, however salutary in itself, could aspire to general recognition. The civil and criminal law, the principles of science, sanitary and police regulations, even the rules of courtesy and decorum, are alike rested on scriptural authority. The entire Talmud may be roughly described as an extended commentary on the Mosaic Law.[1] The authors of the Talmud led a studious life, and relied in great measure upon the habit of study to preserve the vitality of their faith. Among the sayings of the sages[2] we read such as these. Jose ben Joeser says: "Let thy house be the resort of the wise, and let the dust of their feet cover thee, and drink in thirstily their words." Joshua ben Perachia says: "Get thee an instructor, gain a companion [for thy studies], and judge all men upon the presumption of their innocence." Hillel says: "Who gains not in knowledge loses. . . . Say not, 'When I am at leisure I will study'; 't is likely thou wilt never be at leisure. . . . He who increases flesh increases corruption; he who increases worldly goods increases care; he who increases servants increases theft; but he who increases in the knowledge of the Law increases life." Jochanan ben Sakkai says: "If thou art wise in the knowledge of the Law, take not credit to thyself, for to this end wast thou created." After the

---

[1] For a concise but comprehensive account of the origin of the Talmud, vide the art. *Talmud* in Johnson's Encyclopædia.

[2] Collected in the Tract Aboth (Fathers).

destruction of the Temple by Titus, academies sacred to the study of the Law were erected in different cities of Palestine, and similar institutions flourished on the banks of the Euphrates. In the eleventh century the chief seats of Jewish learning were transplanted to the West; and since that time the European Jews have excelled their brethren of the East in all the elements of mental culture. In the course of their manifold wanderings the Jews carried their libraries everywhere with them. Wherever a synagogue arose, a school for young children and a high school for youths were connected with it. In the dark night of the ghetto the flame of knowledge was never quenched. While the nations of Europe were still sunk in barbarism the Jews zealously devoted themselves to the pursuit of medicine, mathematics, and dialectics, and the love of learning became an hereditary quality in their midst. The efforts of many generations have contributed to keep their intellectual faculties bright; and, unlike most oppressed races, they have emerged from a long epoch of systematic persecution well fitted to attack the problems of the present with fresh interest and undiminished capacity.

THE DEMOCRATIC ORGANIZATION OF THE SYNAGOGUE.

The spirit of monotheism is essentially democratic both in politics and religion. There is to be but one king, and he the spiritual Lord in heaven. All the people are equal before him. When the Hebrews clamorously demanded a king the prophet charged them with treason against their proper ruler. The prophet and priest were hostile powers; and their antagonism was clearly felt, and sometimes energetically expressed. The Lord takes no delight in the slaughter of animals. The bloody sacrifices are an offence to Him. What He requires is purity of heart, righteous judgment, and care for the widow and the fatherless. The idea of priestly mediation—of mediation in any shape—was repugnant to the Jews. "The whole people are priests," it was said. When the sanctuary at Jerusalem had been laid in ashes, anything resembling a hierarchical caste was no longer tolerated among them. The Law and the Science of the Law were open to all; and each one was expected, according to the measure of his capacity, to draw directly from the

APPENDIX.

fountain-head of faith. The autonomy of the congregations was strictly guarded. Entire uniformity in the ritual was never achieved.[1] The public lector of prayers was called "the delegate of the congregation." The Rabbies (the word means Masters, in the sense of teachers) were men distinguished for superior erudition and the blamelessness of their lives, and these qualities formed their only title to distinction.[2] Their duties differed radically from those of the Catholic priest or the Protestant clergyman. They never took upon themselves the care of souls. Their office was to instruct the young, and in general to regulate the practice of religion according to the principles and precedents laid down in the sacred traditions of their people. The several congregations were independent of each other. There were no general synods or councils, no graded hierarchy culminating in a spiritual head, no oligarchy of ministers and elders; but rather a federation of small communities, each being a sovereign unit, and connected with the others solely by the ties of a common faith, common sympathies, and common sufferings. Any ten men were competent to form themselves into a congregation, and to discharge all the duties of religion. The fact that this was so proved of the utmost consequence in preserving the integrity of Judaism. The Jews were parcelled out over the whole earth. The body of the people was again and again divided. But in every case the barest handful that remained sufficed to become the nucleus of new organizations. Had the system of Judaism required any one central organ, a blow aimed against this would doubtless have proved fatal to the whole. But by the wise provisions of the federative system the vital power seems to have been equally disseminated over the entire community. Like the worm that is trodden under foot, to which Israel so often likens itself in the Hebrew prayers, the divided members lived a new life of their own, and though apparently crushed beneath the heel of their oppressors, they ever rose again in indestructible vitality.

[1] Vide Zunz Die Ritus.

[2] Many of them supported themselves by following some humble calling, refusing to receive remuneration for their teachings, on the principle that the Law "should not be made a spade to dig with."

APPENDIX.

THE INFLUENCE OF PERSECUTION.

In surveying the history of the Jewish people we find a strange blending of nationalism and cosmopolitism illustrated in their actions and beliefs. They proudly styled themselves the elect people of God, they looked down with a certain contempt upon the Gentile nations, yet they conceived themselves chosen, not on their own account, but for the world's sake, in order to spread the knowledge of the true God among men. They repudiated heathenism, and regarded Trinitarianism as an aberration. In contradistinction to these their mission was to protect the purity of the monotheistic religion until in the millennial age all nations would gather about their "holy Mount." They considered their own continued existence as a people foreordained in the Divine scheme,[1] because they believed themselves divinely commissioned to bring about the eternal happiness of the human race. The centripetal and centrifugal forces of character were thus evenly balanced, and this circumstance contributed not a little to enliven their courage in the face of long-continued adversity. When the independence of Greece was lost, the Greeks ceased to exist as a nation. But the loss of the Temple and the fatherland gave barely more than a passing shock to the national consciousness of the Jews. Easily they acclimatized themselves in every quarter of the globe. The fact of their dispersion was cited by Christianity as a sign of their rejection by God. They themselves regarded it as a part of their mission to be scattered as seed over the whole earth. That they should suffer was necessary, they being the Messianic people! Their prayers were filled with lamentations and the recital of their cruel woes. But they invariably ended with words of promise and confidence in the ultimate fulfillment of Israel's hope. Thus in the very depths of their degradation they were supported by a sense of the grandeur of their destinies, and by the proud consciousness that their sufferings were

---

[1] "Let it not seem strange to you that we should regain our former condition, even though only a single one of us were left, as it is written, 'Fear not, thou worm, Jacob!'"—JUDA HA-LEVI, in the book *Cusari* (twelfth century), iii. 11.

the price paid for the world's spiritual redemption. In the earlier half of the Middle Ages the Jews were still permitted to enjoy a certain measure of liberty. In Spain, France and Germany they lived on amicable terms with their neighbors, they engaged in trade and manufacture, and were allowed to possess landed property. In the tenth and eleventh centuries a great part of the city of Paris was owned by Jews. But at the time of the Crusades a terrible change in the aspect of their affairs took place. The principles embodied in the canonical law had by this time entered into the practice of the European nations. Fanaticism was rampant. The banks of the Rhine and the Moselle became the theatre of the most pitiless persecution. Among the Crusaders the cry was raised, "We go to Palestine to slay the unbelievers; why not begin with the infidel Jews in our own midst?" Worms, Spires, Mayence, Strassburg, Basle, Regensburg, Breslau, witnessed the slaughter of their Jewish inhabitants. Toward the close of the thirteenth century one hundred thousand Jews perished at the hands of Rindfleisch, and the murderous hordes of whom he was the leader. To add fuel to the passions of the populace the most absurd accusations were brought forward against them, and their religion was made odious by connecting it with charges of grave moral obliquity. Jewish physicians being in great request, especially at the court of kings, it was given out that with fiendish malice they were wont to procure the death of their Christian patients.[1] They were accused of killing Christian children, and using the blood of Christians in celebrating the Passover festival, and this monstrous falsehood was repeated until no one doubted its substantial truth. Let it be remembered that this charge was originally preferred, in a somewhat different shape, against the Christians themselves. It floated down, as such rumors will, from age to age, until, its authorship being forgotten, it was finally used as a convenient handle against the hated Jews. In this manner the Easter-tide which was to announce the triumph of a religion of love became to the Jews a season of terror and mortal agony, and the Easter dawn was often reddened with the flames that rose from Jewish homes. It is impossible to calculate the number of lives that

[1] Thus in the case of Charles the Bald, and others.

have been lost in consequence of this single accusation. It has lived on even into the present century.[1] In the fourteenth century the Black Death devastated the Continent of Europe. Soon the opinion gained ground that the Jews were responsible for the ravages of the plague. It was claimed that the Rabbi of Toledo had sent out a venomous mixture concocted of consecrated wafers and the blood of Christian hearts to the various congregations, with orders to poison the wells. The Pope himself undertook to plead for their innocency, but even papal bulls were powerless to stay the popular madness. In Dekkendorf a church was built in honor of the massacre of the Jews of that town, and the spot thus consecrated has remained a favorite resort of pilgrims down to modern times. The preaching friars of the Franciscan and Dominican orders were particularly active in fanning the embers of bigotry whenever they threatened to die down. In England, France and Spain the horrors enacted in Germany were repeated on a scale of similar magnitude. The tragic fate of the Jews of York, the fury of the Pastoureaux, the miserable scenes that accompanied the exodus of the Jews from Spain are familiar facts of history. In Poland, in the seventeenth century, the uprising of the Cossacks under the chieftainship of Chmielnicki became once more the signal of destruction. It is estimated that in ten years (1648–1658) upwards of two hundred and fifty thousand Jews perished.[2] Even when the lives of the Jews were spared, their condition was so extremely wretched that death might often have seemed the preferable alternative. The theory propounded by the Church and acted out by the temporal rulers of the Middle Ages is expressed in the words of

[1] In the year 1840 it was simultaneously renewed in Rhenish Prussia, on the Isle of Rhodos, and in the city of Damascus. In that city the most respected members of the Jewish community were arrested, with the assistance of the French Consul, Ratti Menton, and underwent cruel torture. The intense excitement caused throughout Europe at the time is, doubtless, still fresh in the memory of many who will read these pages. The utter falsity of the charge was at last exposed, thanks to the efforts of the Austrian Consul Merlato and the energetic action of Lord Palmerston.

[2] Graetz, Gesch. der Juden, X. p. 78.

Innocent III., "Quos propria culpa submisit perpetuæ servituti, quum Dominum crucifixerint—pietas Christiana receptet et sustineat cohabitationem illorum."[1]

By the crucifixion of Jesus the Jews had forfeited for themselves and their posterity the right to exist in Christian states. They lived on sufferance merely. In the feudal system there was no room for them. They were aliens, were regarded as the property of the Emperor, and he was free to deal with them as suited his convenience. Hence the name *servi cameræ*—servants of the imperial chamber—was applied to them. They could be sold, purchased, given away at pleasure. Charles IV. presented " the persons and property of his Jews" to the city of Worms. In a schedule of toll-dues dating from the year 1398 we read : "a horse pays two shillings, a Jew six shillings, an ox two heller."[2] They were compelled to wear a badge of shame upon their garments;[3] were confined to narrow and filthy quarters,—*ghetto, juderia,*—debarred from all honorable employments. The schools and universities were closed against them. The guilds shut them out from the various trades. To gain the means of subsistence nothing remained for them but to engage in the petty traffic of the peddler or the disreputable business of the money-lender. They had absolutely no choice in the matter. The laws of Moses certainly discountenance the lending of money at interest. The authorities of the Talmud severely condemn the practice of usury, and refuse to admit the testimony of usurers in courts of law.[4] But all scruples on the part of the Jews had now to be set aside. Gold they must have, and in abundance. It was the only means of buying their peace. The taxes levied by the imperial chamber

---

[1] Cassel, art. *Juden*, p. 83, in Ersch und Gruber ; vide also p. 85, "ad perpetuam Judaici sceleris ultionem eisdem Judæis induxerit perpetuam servitutem."

[2] Ibid, p. 91.

[3] The *signum circulare* was borrowed from Islam. It has been ingeniously conjectured that the circular form was selected in contradistinction to the sign of the crescent. Ibid, p. 75.

[4] Mishna Sanhedrin, III. 3.

were enormous.[1] The cities, the baronial lords, in whose territory they took refuge, constantly imposed new burdens as the price of toleration. The Jews have often been held up to contempt for their avarice and rapacity. The reproach is unjust. It reminds one of the ancient Philistines, who, having shorn the Hebrew of his strength and blinded him, called him with jeers from his prison-house to exhibit him to the popular gaze and to make sport of his infirmity.

Under these circumstances the conservatism of the Jews in matters of religion can no longer astonish us. Rejected by the world, they lived in a world of their own. They had inherited from their ancestors an extended code of ceremonial observances, dietary laws, and minute and manifold directions for the conduct of life. In these they beheld the bulwark of their religion, the common bond that united the scattered members of their race. The Jew of Persia or Palestine could come among his German brethren, and hear the same prayers expressed in the same language, and recognize the same customs as were current among his co-religionists in the East. The passwords of the faith were everywhere understood. To preserve complete unanimity with respect to religious usage was a measure dictated by the commanding instinct of self-preservation. The Jews of all countries were furthermore united by the common yearnings with which they looked back to the past, and their common hope of ultimate restoration to the heritage of the promised land.[2] However prolonged their abode in the land of the stranger might be, they never regarded it otherwise than in the light of a temporary sojourn, and Palestine remained their true fatherland. "If I forget thee, Jerusalem, wither my right

---

[1] A general tax paid in recognition of the Emperor's protection; the Temple tax claimed by the Holy Roman Emperor in his capacity as the successor of Vespasian; the so-called *aurum coronarium*, or coronation tax, by virtue of which every new emperor, upon his accession to the throne, could confiscate the third part of the property of the Jews. Besides these, extraordinary levies were frequent.

[2] On the eve of the 9th of the fifth month it was customary at Jerusalem to announce the number of years that had elapsed since the fall of the Temple. Zunz, Die Ritus, p. 84.

hand," was sung as plaintively on the banks of the Danube and the Rhine as it had resounded of old by Babel's streams. The Jewish people walked through history as in a dream, their eyes fixed on Zion's vanished glories. Empires fell; wars devastated the earth; new manners, new modes of life, arose around them. What was all this toil and turmoil of the nations to them! They were not admitted to the fellowship of mankind, they preserved their iron stability, they alone remained changeless. So long as the world maintained its hostile attitude toward them, there was little likelihood that they would abandon their time-honored traditions. But toward the close of the last century the first tokens of political, social, and spiritual regeneration began to appear among the despondent people of the Hebrews. The spirit of the Reformation, which had slumbered so long, awoke to new vitality. The voice of love rebuked the selfishness of creeds; Philosophy in the person of Kant emphasized the duties of man to man; Poetry sent its warm breath through the German land, and with its sweet strains instilled broad, humanitarian doctrine into the hearts of men. Lessing celebrated the virtues of his friend, Moses Mendelssohn, in "Nathan the Wise," and in the parable of the rings showed how the true religion is to be sought and found. The Royal Academy at Berlin nominated the same Mendelssohn for membership in its body. Jewish scholars were received with distinction in the Austrian and Prussian capitals. Eminent statesmen and writers began to exert themselves to remove the foul blot that had so long stained the conduct of the Christian states in their dealings with the Jews. In France the great Revolution was rapidly sweeping away the accumulated wrongs of centuries. When the emancipation of the Jews came up for discussion in the Convention, the ablest speakers rose in their behalf. The Abbé Gregoire exclaimed: "A new century is about to open. May its portals be wreathed with the palm of humanity!" Mirabeau lent his mighty eloquence to their cause. "I will not speak of tolerance," he said; "the freedom of conscience is a right so sacred that even the name of tolerance involves a species of tyranny."[1] On the 28th September, 1791, the National Con-

[1] Vide the account of the debates in the official Moniteur.

vention decreed the equality of the Israelites of France with their Christian fellow-citizens. The waves of the Revolution, however, overflowed the borders of France, and the agitation they caused was quickly communicated to all Germany. Wherever the armies of the Republic penetrated, the gates of the ghettos were thrown open, and in the name of Fraternity, Liberty and Equality were announced to their inhabitants. When Napoleonic misrule at last exasperated Germany into resistance, the seeds which French influence had sown had already taken firm root in the German soil. On the 11th March, 1812, Frederick William III. issued his famous edict, removing the main disabilities from which the Jews of his dominions had suffered, granting them the rights and imposing upon them the honorable duties of citizenship. They were no longer to be classed as foreigners. The state claimed them as its children, and exacted of them the same sacrifices as all its sons were called upon to bring in the troublous times that soon followed. With what eager alacrity the Jews responded to the king's call the records of the German wars for independence amply testify. On the battlefields of Leipzig and Waterloo they stood side by side with their Christian brethren. Many sons and fathers of Jewish households yielded their lives in the country's defence. In the blood of the fallen the new covenant of equal justice was sealed for all time to come. However prejudice might still dog their footsteps, however shamefully the government might violate its solemn pledges to the Jewish soldiers on their return from the wars, the Jews of Germany had now gained what they could no more lose. They felt that the land for which they had adventured their all, in whose behalf they had lost so much, was indeed their fatherland. For the first time, after many, many centuries, the fugitives had gained a home, a country. They awoke as from a long sleep. They found the world greatly changed around them; vast problems engaging the attention of thinkers, science and philosophy everywhere shedding new light upon the path of mankind. They were eager to approve themselves worthy and loyal citizens, eager to join in the general work of progress. They dwelt no more with anxious preference on the past. The present and the future demanded their exertions, and the motives that had so long compelled their exclusion from the fellowship of the Gentiles were gradually disappearing. As their religion was mainly retrospective in character and exclusive in tendency, great changes were needed to bring it into harmony with the altered condition of affairs. These changes were accordingly attempted, and their history is the history of Jewish Reform.

III.

REFORMED JUDAISM.

REFORMED Judaism originated in Germany; its leading representatives have invariably been Germans. The history of Germany during the past one hundred years is the background upon which our account of the movement must be projected.

The Jews of Germany had waited long and patiently for deliverance. At last, toward the close of the eighteenth century it came, and one whom they delight to call their "Second Moses" arose to lead them into the promised land of freedom. This was Moses Mendelssohn. His distinguished merits as a writer on philosophy and æsthetics we need not here pause to dilate upon, but shall proceed at once to consider him in his relations to the political, social, and religious emancipation of his people. In each of these different directions his example and influence upon others served to initiate a series of salutary changes, and he may thus appropriately be termed the father of the Reform movement in its widest acceptation. It was Mendelssohn who, in 1781, inspired Christian Wilhelm Dohm to publish his book "On the Civil Amelioration of the Jews," a work in which an earnest plea for their enfranchisement was for the first time put forth. The author points to the thrift and frugality that mark the Jewish race, their temperate habits and love of peace, and exposes the folly of debarring so valuable a class of the population from the rights of the citizen. He appeals to the wisdom of the government to redeem the errors and injustice of the past; he defends the Jews against the absurd charges which were still repeated to their discredit, and strenuously insists that liberty and humane treatment would not only accrue to their own advantage, but would ultimately redound to the honor and lasting welfare of the state. Dohm's book created a profound impression, and though it failed to produce immediate results, materially aided the cause of emancipation at a later period.

Again Mendelssohn was the first to break through the social restraints that obstructed the intercourse of Jews and Christians, and thus triumphed over a form of prejudice which is commonly the last to yield. His fame as a writer greatly assisted him in this respect. The grace and freshness of his style, the apparent ease with which he divested the stern problems of philosophy of their harsher aspects, had won him many and sincere admirers. His " Phædon " was eagerly read by thousands, whom the writings of Leibnitz and Kant had repelled. On the afternoon of the Jewish Sabbath he was accustomed to assemble many of the choice spirits of the Prussian capital, among whom we may mention Lessing, Nikolai, and Gleim, in his home. The conversation turned upon the gravest and loftiest topics that can occupy the human soul. The host himself skilfully guided the stream of discussion, and the waves of thought flowed easily along in that placid, restful motion which is adapted to speculative themes. The spirit that of old had hallowed the shades of Academe presided over these gatherings. Mendelssohn emulated the plastic idealism of Plato and the divine hilarity of Socrates. The singular modesty, the truthfulness and quiet dignity that adorned his character were reflected upon the people from whom he had sprung, and produced a salutary change in their favor in the sentiments of the better classes.

But it is as the author of a profound revolution in the Jewish religion that Mendelssohn attracts our especial interest. Not, indeed, that he himself ever assumed the character of a religious reformer. He was, on the contrary, sincerely devoted to the orthodox form of Judaism, and even had a change appeared to him feasible or desirable, he would in all probability have declined the responsibility of publicly advocating it. His was the contemplative spirit which instinctively shrinks from the rude contact of reality. He had neither the aggressive temper nor the bold self-confidence that stamp the leader of parties. And yet, without intending it, he gave the first impulse to Jewish Reform, whose subsequent progress, could he have foreseen it, he would assuredly have been the first to deprecate.

THE BIBLE.

The condition of the Jews at the close of the last century was in many respects unlike that of any other race that has ever been led from a state of subjection to one of acknowledged equality. Long oppression had not, on the whole, either blunted their intellects or debased their morals. If they were ignorant in modern science and literature, they were deeply versed in their own ancient literature, and this species of learning was not the privilege of a single class, but the common property of the whole people. What they lacked was system. In the rambling debates of the Talmud the true principles of logical sequence are but too often slighted, and the student is encouraged to value the subtle play of dialectics on its own account, without regard to any ultimate gain in positive and useful knowledge. Impatience of orderly arrangement being allowed to develop into a habit, became contagious. It impressed itself equally on the thought, the manners, the language[1] of the Jews, and contributed not a little to alienate from them the sympathies of the refined. Such, however, was the preponderating influence of the Talmud that it not only engrossed the attention of the Jewish youth to the exclusion of secular knowledge, but even perverted the exegesis of the Bible and caused the study of Scripture to be comparatively neglected. To weaken the controlling influence of the Talmud became the first needful measure of Reform, and to accomplish this it was necessary to give back to the Bible its proper place in the education of the young. It was an event, therefore, of no mean significance when Mendelssohn, in conjunction with a few friends, determined to prepare a German translation of the Pentateuch, and thus, by presenting the teachings of Scripture in the garb of a modern tongue, to render their true meaning apparent to every reflecting mind. The work was finished in 1783. It holds a like relation to the Jewish Reform movement that Luther's translation held to the great Protestant movement of the sixteenth century. It was greeted with a storm of abuse upon its appearance, and was loudly execrated by the

[1] The German Jews spoke a mixed dialect of German and Hebrew, which has been likened to the so-called Pennsylvania Dutch.

orthodox as the beginning of larger and far-reaching innovations. Its author might sincerely protest his entire innocency of the radical designs imputed to him, but subsequent events have proved the keener insight of his opponents. The influence of the new translation was twofold. In the first place it facilitated a more correct understanding of the doctrine, the literature and language of Scripture; secondly,—and this is worthy of special remark,—it served the purpose of a text-book of the German for the great mass of the Jews, who were at that time unable to read a book written in the vernacular, and thus became the means of opening to them the treasure-house of modern thought.[1] In the very year in which Mendelssohn's work appeared we notice among the younger generation a general revival of interest in the Hebrew, the mother-tongue of their race. Two students of the University of Königsberg began the issue of a periodical devoted to the culture of the Hebrew, which was widely read and attracted great attention. Poems, original essays, Hebrew versions of modern writings, appeared in its columns; the style of the Prophets and of the Psalmists was emulated, the works of the ancient masters of the language served as models, and in the aspect of the noble forms employed in the diction of the biblical authors the æsthetic sense of the modern Jews revived. We are inclined to doubt whether the Hebrew Bible, considered merely with a view to its æsthetic value, is even yet fully appreciated. The extravagance of religious credulity and the violent extreme of scepticism have alike tended to obscure its proper merits. The one accustomed to behold in the "holy book" a message from the Creator to his creatures shrinks, as a rule, from applying to the work of a Divine author the critical standard of human composition. The sceptics on the other hand, impatient of the exorbitant claims which are urged for the sacred writings of the Jews, and resenting the sway which they still exercise over the human reason, are hardly in a proper frame of mind to estimate justly its intrinsic and imperishable excellences. And yet, setting aside all questions of the supernatural origin of the Bible, and regarding

[1] The German of Mendelssohn's translation was written in Hebrew letters.

only the style in which its thoughts are conveyed, how incomparably valuable does it still remain! It would be difficult to calculate the extent to which many of our standard authors are indebted for the grandest passages of their works to their early familiarity with the biblical style. Those who are able to read the text in the original become aware of even subtler beauties that escape in the process of translation. Purity of diction, power of striking antithesis, simple and yet sublime imagery, a marvellous facility in the expression of complex states of feeling, and those the deepest of which the human soul is capable, are but a few of the obvious features that distinguish the golden age of Hebrew literature. Never perhaps has the symbolism of nature been used with such supreme effect to express the unspeakable emotions that are deep down in the heart of man. Such music as that which swells through the pages of Isaiah's prophecies cannot be forgotten; such ringing, rhythmic periods, in which the eloquence of conviction bursts forth into the rounded fulness of perfect oratory, can never fail to touch and to inspire. We know of no nobler pattern on which the modern orator could mould his style. And thus, too, the exquisite poetry of the Song of Songs, the idyl of the Book of Ruth, the weird pathos of Jeremiah's lament, the grand descriptions of Job, will ever be counted among the masterpieces of human genius. Whatever we may think of the doctrines of the Bible, it is safe to predict that the book will live long after the myths that surround its origin shall have been dispelled; nay, all the more, when it shall cease to be worshipped as a fetish will men appreciate its abiding claims to their reverence, and it will continue to hold its honored place in the libraries of the nations. The refining influence of the study of the Bible soon became evident among the contemporaries of Mendelssohn. But in another way also his translation tended to their improvement. We have said that it became the means of acquainting them with the language of the land. A wide field of knowledge, embracing the rich results of modern science, philosophy, and art, was thus laid open to their industry. Eagerly they availed themselves of the proffered opportunity; schools were erected, in which the elements of liberal culture were imparted to the young, and ere long we find a new generation of the Jews engaging in honorable competition with their Christian brethren for the prize of learning and the rewards of literary distinction. It was at this time that Kant's "Critique of Pure Reason" appeared, a work which marks a new epoch in the world's thought. Its profound reasoning and technical style made it difficult of comprehension to all but the initiated. Three Jewish scholars—Dr. Herz, Salomon Maimon, and Ben-David—undertook the task of popularizing its main results, and were among the first to call attention to the transcendent importance of the new system. Plainly new vital energy was coursing through the veins of the Jewish people.

SOCIAL STANDING.

But at this very time, while they were rapidly assimilating the best results of modern culture and winning the respect and confidence of the learned, the Jews of Germany were still laboring under an odious system of special laws, and beheld themselves excluded from the common rights of citizenship. The manly effort of Dohm in their behalf had as yet availed nothing; the voice of bigotry was still supreme in the councils of the sovereign. And yet they felt themselves to be the equals of those whom the law unjustly ranked their superiors, and longed to see the barriers done away that still divided them from their fellow-men. Many of their number had amassed fortunes, and expended their wealth with commendable prudence and generosity. They supported needy students, founded libraries, extended their knowledge, and refined their tastes. Even the Jewish maidens followed the general impulse toward self-culture that was setting with such force in the Jewish community. In particular the works of Schiller and Goethe, as they successively appeared at this period, inflamed their enthusiasm, and none were more zealous than they in spreading the fame and influence of the new school of German literature. Still they were taught to consider themselves an inferior class, and were despised as such. The position of equality which the narrowness of the laws denied them they were resolved to achieve by the weight of character and the force of spiritual attractions. Henrietta de

Lemos, a young girl of singular beauty and attainments, had at this time become the wife of Dr. Herz, of whom we have casually spoken above in his connection with Kant. She is described as tall, graceful, possessing a face in which the features of Hellenic and Oriental beauty were blended in exquisite harmony ; while the sobriquet of the "Tragic Muse," by which she became known, denoted the majestic nobleness of her presence. Under the guidance of competent masters she had acquired considerable proficiency in many of the modern and ancient languages, and to a mind stored with various knowledge was added the mellow charm of a most sweet and loving disposition. Attracted by her fame and captivated by her genius, the most eminent men of the day sought the privilege of her society. The art of conversation, which had till then received but little attention in the Prussian capital, was for the first time cultivated in the *salon* of Henrietta Herz. Sparkling wit and profound philosophy were alike encouraged. Statesmen high in the service of their country sought the amenities of these delightful gatherings. Alexander and Wilhelm von Humboldt, Gentz, Schleiermacher, Friedrich von Schlegel, Mirabeau, Dorothea, the daughter of Mendelssohn, Rahel, afterwards wife of Varnhagen von Ense, were among the intimates of her circle. Christians and Jews met here on terms of mutual deference, and forgot for a while the paltry distinctions which still kept them asunder in the world without. And yet these distinctions, senseless in themselves, were full of ominous meaning to those who felt their burden. Young men eager for advancement in life found their religion an insuperable obstacle in their way. The professions, the army, the offices of the government, were closed against them. On the threshold of every higher career they were rudely repulsed, unless they embraced the base alternative of changing their creed to satisfy their ambition. Under these circumstances that fidelity to the faith of the fathers which had so long marked the conduct of the Jews began seriously to waver, and in many instances gave way. Not, indeed, that the new converts became true and loyal Christians. On the contrary, they considered the rite of baptism a mere hollow form, and left it to the state, which had insisted upon their conformance, to justify the deep disgrace that was thus brought upon the Christian sacraments. Moreover, a certain laxity in the interpretation of dogma had at this time become widely prevalent, which greatly assisted them in setting their conscience at ease. Rationalism had stripped the positive religions of much of their substance and individuality. To none of them was an absolute value allowed. They were regarded as forms in which a principle higher than all forms had found an imperfect and temporary expression. Even the influence of Schleiermacher tended rather to obliterate than to define the outlines of the contending creeds. Schleiermacher, the author of a Protestant revival in Germany, spoke the language of Pantheism, and his opinions are deeply suffused with the spirit of Pantheistic teachings. He defines religion to be the sense of dependence on the Infinite, the Universal. To the fact that different men in different ages have been variously affected by the conception of the Infinite he ascribes the origin of the different creeds. Theological dogmas, according to him, cannot claim to be true in the sense of scientific or philosophical propositions. They approach the truth only in so far as they typically express certain emotional processes of our soul, and those dogmas are nearest the truth which typify emotions of the most noble and exalted character. Allowing Christianity to be what its learned expounders had defined it, intelligent Jews could hardly find it difficult to assume the Christian name. It is estimated that in the course of three decades full one half of the Jewish community of Berlin were nominally Christianized.

How thoroughly conventional, at the same time, the use of the term Christian had become may be judged from a letter addressed by David Friedlander, a friend of Mendelssohn's, to Councillor Teller of the Consistory, in which he offered, on behalf of himself and some co-religionists, to accept Christianity in case they might be permitted to omit the observance of the Christian festivals, to reject the doctrine of the Trinity, of the divinity of Jesus, and, in fact, whatever is commonly regarded as essentially and specifically Christian. It is true the reply of the Councillor was not encouraging.

PARIS, THE NEW JERUSALEM.

While the very existence of Judaism was thus threatened in Germany, it seemed about to regain its pristine vigor in France. More than seventeen centuries had elapsed since the Sanhedrin, the High Court of Jerusalem, had passed out of existence. Quite unexpectedly it was recalled to momentary life by the caprice of the great Corsican, who then ruled the destinies of the world. In the year 1806 Napoleon convened a parliament of Jewish Notables at Paris in order to definitely settle the relations of French Israelites to the state. Soon after an imperial decree convoked the grand Sanhedrin for the purpose of ratifying the decisions of the Notables. The glories of Jerusalem were to be renewed in "modern Babylon" on the Seine. On February 9, 1807, the Sanhedrin met in the Hotel de Ville. Care was taken to invest its sittings with due solemnity; the seats of the members were arranged in crescent shape about the platform of the presiding officers, as had been customary at Jerusalem; the president was saluted with the title of Nassi (Prince), as in the olden time; the ancient titles and forms were copied with scrupulous exactness. Two-thirds of the members were Rabbis, the remainder laymen. The opening of the Sanhedrin attracted universal attention, but its proceedings were void of interest. In fact, its sole task was to lend the authority of an ancient tribunal to the action of the Notables, and this having been accomplished it was adjourned after a brief session. In connection with these conventions of the years 1806 and 1807 it behooves us to mention the creation of a new constitution for the French synagogue elaborated by the joint efforts of the imperial Commissioners and the Notables. The form of government adopted was moulded on the pattern of the secular power. A system of consistories was organized throughout France, culminating in a central consistory at Paris with a Grand-Rabbin at its head. The officers of the consistories were treated as officers of the state, the charge of their maintenance was in part defrayed at the public expense, and, in the course of time, they were placed on a footing of almost complete equality with the dignitaries of the Christian churches. The union of the teachers of Judaism in a species of graded hierarchy, dependent upon temporal rulers for their support, was as have have been expected, fruitful of evil results. If it is true that the supremacy of the church over the state disturbs the peace of nations and endangers the very existence of governments, it is equally certain that no religion can long continue to maintain its purity when the church becomes the subservient vassal of the state. Whatever the apparent gain in stability may be, it is more than counterbalanced by the loss of spontaneity and sincerity. Hypocrisy flourishes, the liberty of conscience is abridged, and a spirit of base time-serving eventually prepares the downfall of institutions whose perfect safety is consistent only with perfect freedom.

The French Synagogue, as we have indicated, presents a case in point. During the past seventy years it has stagnated. No single luminous thought lights up its dreary record, no single whole-souled effort to appropriate the larger truths of our time dignifies its annals. In the history of the Reform movement it merits no further mention.

THE LITURGY.

Returning to Germany we behold the leading Jews at last awakened to the necessity of energetic measures to check the wide-spread disaffection that was thinning out their ranks. Hitherto the liturgy of the synagogue had not been affected by the growing tendency to change. An attempt in this direction was initiated by Israel Jacobsohn, the financial agent of the Duke of Brunswick, a man of wealth, culture, and generous disposition. He was shocked by the scenes of disorder, the utter lack of decorum, that disgraced the public worship; he was resolved as far as in his power lay to correct the abuses which had been allowed to grow up unrestrained in the gloomy period of mediæval persecution, and to win back to the faith those whose affections had been estranged by the barbarous form in which it appeared to view. He erected at his own expense, and dedicated on July 17, 1810, in the town of Seesen, a new temple,[1] at the same time in-

---

[1] The term Temple has since been used by the Reformers in contradistinction to the orthodox Synagogue.

troducing certain radical modifications into the service which we shall presently take occasion to consider.

Being appointed to the Presidency of the Consistory of Cassel, during the reign of Jerome Bonaparte, he took advantage of his official position to urge his innovations upon the congregations under his charge. In 1815 he transplanted the "new fashion in religion" to Berlin, and in 1818 assisted in founding the temple at Hamburg, which soon became one of the leading strongholds of Reform. A provisional service on the same plan was likewise instituted at Leipsic,[1] during the period of the annual fair, and tidings of the reform were thus rapidly transmitted to distant parts of Germany. The main changes introduced by Jacobsohn, and copied by others, may be briefly summed up as follows : The introduction of regular weekly sermons, which had not previously been customary ; of prayers in the vernacular by the side of the Hebrew ; of choir singing with organ accompaniment, and the confirmation of young children. These innovations implied a revolution in the character of the public worship.

The Jewish people had been wont to regard themselves individually and collectively, as soldiers in the army of their God, commissioned to wage warfare against every species of false religion. A spirit of martial discipline, as it were, pervaded their ranks. The repetition of prayers and benedictions by day and night in the privacy of domestic life, on the public square and by the roadside, was a species of drill intended to keep alive in them the consciousness of their mission, and to prepare them for the emergencies of actual conflict. Thrice a day they mustered in their synagogues, and renewed their oath of allegiance in the presence of their spiritual king. The term Jewish Church, though in frequent use, is a misnomer based upon false analogy. The difference between the synagogue and the church is as clearly marked as that between Judaism and Christianity themselves. The sentimental element, using the word in its nobler signification, which is distinctive of the latter, is almost entirely lacking in the former. Both make it their aim to elevate the moral life in man, but while Judaism acts through the will upon

[1] Dr. Zunz was appointed preacher, and the composer Meyerbeer directed the musical services.

the affections, Christianity places the affections in the foreground and seeks by their means to persuade and captivate the will.

It cannot be denied that the Reformers had in some measure modified the traditional character of Jewish worship. The purely emotional element acquired a prominence which it had never had before, the very word employed to designate the purpose of the temple service—"Erbauung," edification—was foreign to the ancient vocabulary of Judaism. In another direction, too, they transgressed the limits prescribed by time-honored usage. We have referred above to the ceremony of confirmation, which has since been generally adopted by congregations of the Reform school. On some festival or Sabbath—the Feast of Weeks, celebrated about Whitsuntide, being commonly preferred—boys and girls of thirteen or fourteen are assembled in the temple, where, after having undergone an examination in the chief tenets of their religion, they are required to repeat aloud a confession of faith. The ceremony usually attracts a large congregation, and is one of the few institutions introduced by the Reformers that have strongly seized upon the popular heart.

The natural concern of parents for the welfare of their offspring lends a solemn interest to the occasion. At an age when the child's character begins to assume definite outlines, when the reason unfolds, and the perils and temptations that attend every pilgrim on the valley road of life, approach near, an instinctive prompting of the human heart leads us to forecast the future of sons and daughters, and to embrace with joy whatever means are placed at our disposal to guard them against aberration and misfortune. To utilize the impressiveness of a great public gathering, the sympathetic presence of parents and friends, the earnest monitions of a wise and revered teacher, in order to confirm them in every virtuous endeavor and high resolve, is therefore fit and proper.[1] The propriety of exacting a formal confes-

---

[1] It deserves to be noted that the ceremony of confirmation among the Jews took its origin in the schools of Seesen, Frankfort-on-the-Main, etc. Indeed, the first Reformed congregations were formed by natural accretion about these schools. The influence of schools in giving character and stability to new religious movements is a subject of sufficient importance to deserve separate treatment.

sion of faith, however, has been hotly disputed both by the orthodox and the more advanced liberals. It is urged that Judaism is a practical, rather than a dogmatical religion. Even the existence of a God is rather presupposed as a fact than asserted as a matter of belief. Apart from this it is claimed that a child at thirteen can hardly be prepared to comprehend the fundamental questions of religion, much less to express convictions on problems so grave and difficult. The age of reflection and consequently of doubt is yet to come, nor can any child on the day of its confirmation answer for its convictions ten years thereafter.

The progress of the Reform movement was thus of a character to awaken distrust and fierce contention at every step. The conservative party were enraged at what they considered unwarrantable encroachments upon the traditions of an immemorial past. The radicals were dissatisfied with the lack of substance and vitality in the teachings of the Reformers, the shallow moralizing tone of their preachers, the superficial views of Judaism which they scattered among the multitude.

It may indeed be asked how could better things have been expected at that time. The great facts of Jewish history were not yet clearly known, the philosophy of Judaism was proportionately vague and uncertain. No Jewish author had ever undertaken to write out the annals of his people; chaotic confusion reigned in their chronicles. To know what Judaism might be it seemed necessary to ascertain in the first instance what it had been; the past would prove the index of the future. Untoward events that happened at this period gave a powerful impulse to historical research, and led to fruitful investigations in the domain of Judaism.

"HEP-HEP."

The great battles of 1813 and 1815, in which the German people regained their independence, effected a marvellous change in the spirits and sentiments of the nation.

Accustomed for a long time to endure in silence the insults and arrogance of a foreign despot, they had learned to despair of themselves; a deadly lethargy held their energies in bondage and in the fairy visions of poetry and the daring dreams of metaphysical speculation they sought consolation for the pains and burdens of reality. The victories of Leipsic and Waterloo completely altered the tone of their feelings. It is a not uncommon fact that individuals usually the reverse of self-asserting exhibit, on occasions, an overweening self-consciousness, which is all the more pointed and aggressive because of their secret and habitual self-distrust. We note with curious interest the recurrence of the same obnoxious trait in the life of a great nation. The novel sense of power intoxicated them, the German mind for the moment lost its poise; Romanticism flourished, the violence of the Middle Ages was mistaken for manhood, and held up to the emulation of the present generation. Whatever was German was therefore esteemed good; whatever was foreign was therefore despised, or at best ignored.

The Jews were made to feel the sharp sting of this feverish vanity; their Asiatic origin was cast up against them, though it might have been supposed that a residence of fifteen centuries had given them some claim to dwell at peace with the children of the soil. In the year 1819 the assassination of Kotzebue added fresh fuel to the fervor of Teutonic passion. In August of that year a professor of Wurzburg, who had written in defence of the Jews, was publicly insulted by the students. A tumult ensued, the cry "Hep-Hep"[1] arose on every side, and "Death to the Jews" was the watchword. On the next day the magistrate ordered them to leave Wurzburg, and four hundred in number they were driven beyond the city's limits. Similar excesses occurred in Frankfort-on-the-Main, Meiningen, Carlsruhe, and elsewhere. Inflammatory pamphlets contributed to increase the excitement.

Grattenauer, Rühs, Fries, had written to good effect. All the old falsehoods were revived, the fable of the use of Christian blood at Passover among the rest. It seemed as though the genius of chivalry which the Romantic school had invoked had returned with its grim attendant train to renew the orgies of

[1] "Hep-Hep" has been explained as an abbreviation of the words "Hierosolyma est perdita" (Jerusalem is perished). Probably it is no more than one of those meaningless exclamations which are not infrequent in college jargon.

mediæval persecution in the full light of the nineteenth century. In November appeared the "Judenspiegel," by Hundt-Radowsky. In this the author argues that the murder of a Jew is neither criminal nor sinful. In order to avoid unnecessary bloodshed however, he proposes a more peaceful means of ridding the German people of "these vermin." His propositions, couched in plain language and delivered in sober earnest, are simply these: the men to be castrated, and sold as slaves to the East Indies; the women—but the pen refuses to record the fiendish suggestion. It is mortifying to reflect that this infamous publication was widely circulated and eagerly read.[1]

THE SCIENCE OF JUDAISM.

The sole reply which these occurrences elicited from the intelligent members of the Jewish community was a more strenuous effort on their part to complete the work of inward purification, and renewed zeal in the study of their historic past. They trusted that the image of Judaism, if presented in its proper light, would remove the odium which rested upon their people, and would furthermore become their sure guide in the work of reconstructing the religion of their ancestors.

Late in the year 1819 a "Society for the Culture and Science[2] of the Jews" was founded at Berlin. Its object was twofold: first to promote a more effective prosecution of the "Science of Judaism"; secondly, to elevate the moral tone of the people, to counteract their prevailing bias toward commerce, and to encourage them in the pursuits of agriculture, the trades, and such of the professions as they had access to.

The science of Judaism embraces the departments of history, philosophy, and philology, the last being of special importance, since it presents the key to the correct understanding of the two former. The means adopted to secure these objects were chiefly three,—a scientific institute, a journal whose columns were enriched by many contributions of enduring value, and a school in

[1] Graetz, Geschichte der Juden, X. p. 361.

[2] Throughout this article we use the word "science" in the sense of the German *Wissenschaft*.

which instruction was imparted gratis to poor students and artisans. Among the members of the society we mention Edward Gans, the President, afterwards Professor of Jurisprudence at the University of Berlin; the eminent critic, Dr. Zunz; the poet, Heinrich Heine;[1] Moser; the noble Wholwill; and others.

Unfortunately, the public mind was not yet prepared to appreciate the labors of these men; the society languished for want of support, and after a few years its formal organization was dissolved. But in the brief term of its existence it had accomplished its main object; the science of Judaism was securely established, and it could safely be left to the industry of a few gifted individuals to cultivate and propagate it. The ten years following the "Hep-Hep" excitement witnessed a series of literary achievements whose importance it would be difficult to overrate. Zunz and Rappoport, the pioneers of the new science, discovered the thread by which they were enabled to push their way through the labyrinth of Jewish literature. Profound erudition, critical acumen, and a subtle insight amounting almost to intuition, are displayed in their writings. A band of worthy disciples followed their lead. The chain of tradition, which had seemed hopelessly tangled, was unravelled; many of its missing links were ingeniously supplied, and the sequence of events, on the whole, satisfactorily determined. The dimness and vagueness that had hung over the history of the Jews was giving way, and the leading figures in the procession of past generations assumed clear and distinct outlines. At this time Jost was employed in wirting the first connected history of his people which had ever emanated from Jewish sources.

SCIENTIFIC THEOLOGY.

While scholars were thus busy preparing the way for a new theory of Judaism based on the facts of its history, no efforts were made to press the needful work of practical reform. Indeed, the hostile attitude of the temporal rulers discouraged any

[1] Heine was for some time an instructor in the society's school. For an account of the *Cultur-Verein*, and of the poet's cordial interest in its success, *vide* Strodtmann, "Heine's Leben und Werke," p. 237.

APPENDIX.

such undertaking. The influence of Metternich swayed the councils of the German princes. The King of Prussia had broken the promise of constitutional government which he had given to his people in the hour of need. The power of the Triple Alliance was prepared to crush out the faintest stirrings of political or religious liberty wherever they appeared.

In 1830, however, the revolution in France swept away a second time the throne of the Bourbons, and changed the face of affairs. The courage of the liberal party revived everywhere; the bonds of despotism were relaxed; a spirit of resistance to oppression arose, and grew in intensity from year to year, until it at last found vent in the convulsions of 1848. The Jews felt the prophetic promise of a better order of things, and roused themselves to renewed exertions.

We have indicated in a previous article that the cause of political and of religious emancipation, so far at least as Germany was concerned, advanced in parallel lines. In 1831 Gabriel Riesser addressed a manifesto to the German people on the position of the Jews among them.[1] It was a clear and forcible presentment of the case. The style is dignified, free from the taint of undue self-assertion, and equally free from misplaced modesty. He did not petition for a favor; he demanded a right. He disdained all measures of compromise; he dared to treat the question as one of national importance; he asked for simple justice, and would be content with nothing less. The German people rewarded his manliness with their confidence,[2] and under his able leadership the struggle for emancipation was finally brought to a triumphant close.

In 1835 Abraham Geiger, then Rabbi of Wiesbaden, began the publication of a "Scientific Journal for Jewish Theology," and with the appearance of this periodical the Reform movement entered into its present phase. It was the purpose of Geiger and his coadjutors to prosecute the work of religious renovation on the basis of the science of Judaism. This is the distinguish-

[1] Ueber die Stellung der Bekenner des Mosaischen Glaubens an die Deutschen aller Confessionen. Riesser's Works, II.

[2] He was elected Vice-President of the first German Parliament that met in the Pauls-Kirche in Frankfort.

ing feature of the modern school of Jewish Reform. But, before we proceed to sketch the principles of these "scientific theologians," let us rapidly advert to the brief series of events that mark the outward development of the new school.

Around the standard which Geiger had unfurled a body of earnest men soon collected, who agreed with him in the main in desiring to reconcile science and life (*Wissenschaft und Leben*). They were mostly young men, fresh from the universities, profoundly versed in Hebrew and rabbinic lore, zealous lovers of their religion, equipped with the elements of ancient and modern culture, and anxious to harmonize the conflicting claims of both in their private lives and public station. Many of them underwent severe privations for their convictions' sake. They were distrusted by the various governments, without whose sanction no Jewish clergyman could enter upon his functions, and were made to feel, in common with other Liberals, the displeasure which their measures, moderate though they were, had provoked in high quarters. They were subjected to numberless petty annoyances, and even downright force was employed to check their growing popularity. With the accession of Frederick William IV., the Ultramontanes and the party of retrogression in the Protestant Church completely gained the ascendant.

Covered by the shield of royal favor they offered the most audacious insults to the conscience and common-sense of the people, the right of free speech was impaired, the press was shackled, while the most abject superstitions were openly encouraged. The holy coat of Jesus, exhibited at the cathedral of Treves, attracted hundreds of thousands of pilgrims, and the fame of the miraculous cures it had effected was diligently spread. But the very violence of the extremists provoked a determined opposition among the intelligent classes. National unity and individual liberty were loudly demanded, a German Catholic party was formed with the avowed object of reorganizing Catholicism on the basis of the modern State. Free religious congregations began to crop up here and there, which, though feeble as yet in their organization, were properly regarded as significant of the spirit of the times. On the waves of the turning tide the young Rabbis were carried along. They, too, were ardent patriots; they, too, were eager to see their religion wedded to the progressive tendencies of the age. The sympathies of the most enlightened of their brethren were cheerfully extended to them, and high hopes were founded on their success.

In 1844 they were sufficiently strong to meet in convention. Disclaiming the functions of a religious synod, they assumed the character of a scientific body, assembled to promote the objects of truth in their special department. The discussions were indeed intended to secure harmony of sentiment and action, but the resolutions adopted were binding neither upon the members themselves nor upon the congregations they represented. Three times these conventions were repeated at Brunswick, Frankfort, and Breslau.

In 1845 a new congregation was formed, called "The Reform Association of Berlin," which was recruited from the extreme left wing of the liberal Jewish party. This congregation became noted for the introduction of a Sunday service, a measure which eventually compelled them to entirely abandon the Jewish Sabbath. Samuel Holdheim, the ablest exponent of radical Judaism, was selected to be their preacher.

Thus far had the Reform movement proceeded, when, in 1848, the incidents of a great political revolution crowded every other issue into comparative insignificance. The fall of Metternich before the intrigues of the camarilla and the fury of a popular uprising, the humiliation of the king of Prussia, the convocation of the national parliament, the Baden insurrection,—these were the events that absorbed the interest of the public. Political incompetency on the part of the leaders precipitated the catastrophe of the revolution, and the hopes of the German people were again doomed to disappointment. Soon the reaction set in, a dreary period of stagnation followed, and the efforts of the friends of freedom were paralyzed.

The Jewish Reformers were stricken down by the general reverse that had overtaken the liberal party, nor have they since been able to recover from its stunning effects. Two revolutions, those of 1830 and 1848, mark the growth and the decline of "scientific reform." Within the past thirty years a number of prominent reformers have been called to this country, and to them is due the spread of the movement in the United States.

APPENDIX. 237

The difficulties which confronted them here were of the most formidable kind. The great bulk of the Jewish emigration to the United States were originally drawn from the village congregations of the Fatherland, and were by no means fair specimens of the intelligence and culture of the Jewish race. While they displayed the qualities of energy, perseverance, and thrift, and soon acquired wealth and influence in the commercial world, few only were fitted to appreciate a movement so thoroughly intellectual in its bearings as that which the reformers came to propagate amongst them. The mere externals of reform were readily adopted, but its spiritual essence escaped them. Accordingly, the development of Reformed Judaism on American soil presents no novel or striking features for our consideration, and it may appropriately be treated as a mere offshoot of the German stock.

PRINCIPLES.

Ever since the appearance of Geiger's "Scientific Journal," Jewish philology and Jewish theology have been inseparably connected. To attempt a detailed account of the latter would involve the necessity of frequent reference to the former, an attempt in which we can hardly assume the reader's interest would bear us out. Unwilling to test his patience by such a course, we shall content ourselves with stating the main principles of Reformed Judaism, and briefly indicating the successive steps by which it advanced to its present positions.

The one great fact which the Science of Judaism has indisputably established was the fact of evolution in the sphere of the Jewish religion. Each generation had legislated for itself. The authorities of the Middle Ages had introduced changes in the ritual; the Talmud itself, that corner-stone of orthodoxy, was a stupendous innovation on the simplicity of Bible rthe eligion.[1] Applying the theory of evolution to their own case, the modern

---

[1] The theory of an Oral Law, delivered to Moses on Sinai and handed down from generation to generation, until it was finally embodied in the ordinance of the Talmudical academies, is a palpable fiction, invented by the Talmudists in order to lend to their own decisions the sanction of Divine authorship.

APPENDIX.

Rabbis assumed on their part the right to institute whatever changes the exigencies of the age had rendered imperative. The very fact of change, it is true, presupposes the existence of a substratum that remains unchangeable. What that substratum in the case of Judaism is claimed to be, we shall presently discover. The measures of the Reformers were in the main dictated by the sentiment of patriotism and the desire to remove the barriers that interposed between them and their fellow-men. They would cease to be a "state within the state," cease to separate themselves from the fellowship of the Gentiles. Hence the leading proposition upon which Reformed Judaism is founded. *The Jewish people have ceased to be a national unit, and will exist hereafter as a confederation of religious societies.*

If the Jews have ceased to be a nation, then the Reformers must abandon the idea of a national restoration. They did so. If they have ceased to be a nation, they must give up the hope of a personal Messiah who should lead them back to the promised land. They did so. If they desired no longer to dwell in seclusion they must abolish the dietary laws, which forbid them to taste of the food of Christians, though commanded by the Talmud and founded apparently on the authority of Moses. This, too, they were willing to do. Other changes were inspired by the philosophic teachings of the day, and were undertaken with equal readiness. Thus the doctrine of resurrection in the flesh was set aside. The fabric of ceremonial observances had been rudely shaken, and soon gave way altogether. Changes in the ritual followed. The prayer-book reflected the gloomy spirit of a people whose life was embittered by constant trials and dangers. Naturally they had turned to the past and the glories of Zion ; the pomp of the sacrifices, the advent of the Messiah, the future restoration of the kingdom of David, were the themes on which they loved to dwell. All this was no longer suited to the temper of the modern Jews, and radical alterations became necessary. Many of the festivals and fast-days also were struck from the calendar. One of the most distinctive customs of the Jews, the so-called rite of Abraham's Covenant, was boldly attacked, and though the abolition of this ancient practice is still strenuously resisted, there is little doubt that it will ultimately go with the rest. Samuel Holdheim advocated the propriety of intermarriage between Jews and Christians.

The manner in which these conclusions were reached may be described as follows. At first an attempt was made to found each new measure of Reform on the authority of the Talmud. The Talmud was attacked with its own weapons. The fallacy of such a method becoming apparent, the authority of the Talmud was entirely set aside. A return to the Bible was next in order. But even the laws of the Bible proved to be no longer capable of fulfilment in their totality. A distinction was therefore drawn between the letter and the spirit of the Bible. The letter is man's handiwork, the spirit alone ought to be regarded as the Divine rule of faith. The "spirit of the Bible" is the essence of Judaism, which cannot change. In the process of evolution it constantly assumes new forms, but remains substantially the same. Nor could any motives of expediency, nor could even the ardent desire of political emancipation have induced the Reformers to pursue the course they did, had they for one moment believed it contrary to the substantial teachings of the Bible. The spirit of the Bible is expressed in two fundamental propositions: the existence of one God, the author and governor of the universe; and the Messianic mission of the people of Israel. The former is no longer the exclusive property of Judaism, the latter is distinctively its own; both together express the simple creed of the Reformers.

PROSPECTS.

If now we cast a glance upon the present aspect of Reformed Judaism we are confronted by a state of affairs that by no means corresponds to the great anticipations which were connected with the movement in its earlier stages. The ancient institutions have been cleared away,—that was unavoidable; they had long been tottering to their ruin,—but an adequate substitute for what was taken has not been provided. The leaders have penetrated to the foundations of their religion, but upon these bare foundations they have erected what is at best a mere temporary structure incapable of affording them permanent shelter and protection. The temper of the Reform school has been critical. Its members were admirably fitted to analyze and to dissect; their scholarship is unquestionably great; the stainless purity of their lives has elevated the character of their people and entitled them to sincere respect. But they lacked the constructive genius needed for the creation of new institutions. In the year 1822 Wholwill declared that "the Jews must raise themselves and their principle to the level of science. Science is the one bond that alone can unite the whole human race." The emphasis thus placed on science has continued to distinguish the Reform movement down to the present day. In the sphere of religion, however, it is not sufficient to apprehend the abstract truth of ideas with the help of intellect, but it is necessary to array these ideas in concrete forms, in order that they may warm the heart and stimulate the will.

We hold it erroneous to believe that the age of symbolism is passed. The province of religion is to bring the human soul into communion with the Infinite. In the lower religions the conception of the Infinite was meagre and insufficient and the symbols in use proportionately gross. At the present day it is the ideal of moral perfection that alone is capable of exciting our devotion and kindling our enthusiasm. Now it is true that the material symbolism of the churches and the synagogues, the venerabile, the bread and wine, the scrolls of the Pentateuch tricked out in fanciful vestments, fail to appeal to the sympathies of many educated men and women of our time; not, however, because they are symbols, but because they are inadequate symbols, because of an almost painful disparity between their earthy origin and the vastness of the spiritual ideas which they are intended to suggest. There is, on the other hand, a species of symbolism peculiarly adapted to the needs of the present generation, and which, if properly understood, might be employed to incalculable advantage in the interest of a revival of the religious sentiment. We allude to the symbolism of association.

The tendency to associate the efforts of individuals in corporate action has never been more markedly displayed than in our own day. So long as such associations confine themselves to certain finite objects, they are mere social engines organized with a view to utility and power, and with such we are not concerned. The characteristic of symbols is their suggestiveness. They have a meaning in themselves, but they suggest illimitable meanings beyond their scope. Now a form of organization is not only conceivable, but has actually been attempted, that fully meets the requirements of the symbolic character. The Christian Church is designed to be such an organization. Not only does it propose to unite its members and to satisfy their spiritual needs during the term of their sojourn on earth, but it aspires to typify the union of all saints under the sovereignty of Jesus, and thus to give to the believer a presentiment of the felicity and perfection of the higher world. In like manner the Hebrews have been acquainted with the symbolism of association from a very early period of their history. If they delight to style themselves the chosen people, the meaning of that phrase, so often misunderstood, is purely symbolical.

Recognizing the fact that the majority of mankind are at no time prepared to entertain the ideals of the few, they undertook to work out among themselves a nobler conception of religion and a loftier morality, trusting that the force of their example would in the end bring about the universal adoption of their faith and ethical code. In this sense the choice of Israel was interpreted by the Prophets. They believed that their selection by the Deity imposed upon them heavier responsibilities, and regarded it in the light of an obligation rather than a privilege. What the statue is to the ideal of beauty, a whole people resolved to be in relation to the ideal of the good. The same conception still dominates the thoughts of the Reformers, and is expressed by them in their doctrine of Israel's messianic mission. They claim that the Jews have been for the past three thousand years the " Swiss guard of monotheism." They still believe themselves to be the typical people, and their firm persuasion on this head is the one strong feature of the Reformers' creed. If they will use their world-wide association to illustrate anew the virtues for which their race became renowned in the past,—and we refer especially to the purity of the sexual relations among them, their pious reverence for domestic ties,—they may still become, as they aspire to do, exemplars of purity to be joyfully imitated by others. If they will use it in the spirit of their ancient lawgiver

---

[1] Leviticus xxv. 8.

to tone down the harsh distinctions of wealth and poverty, to establish juster relations between the strong and weak, in brief, to harmonize the social antagonisms of modern life, they may confer an inestimable benefit upon mankind. But the manner in which the symbolism of association might be applied to invigorate the religious sentiment, and to expel the coldness of the times by the fervor of a new enthusiasm, is a subject of too vast dimensions to be thus summarily despatched, and we shall hope to recur to it on some future occasion.[1]

The present condition of liberal Judaism is strongly akin to that of liberal Christianity. The old is dead, the new has not been born. It is hardly safe to predict what possible developments the future may yet have in store. As regards the Jews, however, it is right to add that such changes as have taken place in the constitution of their religion have not brought them in any sense nearer to Christianity. On the contrary, since the belief in a personal Messiah has been dropped, the hope of their conversion has become more vague and visionary than ever. Those whom the worship of the synagogue and the temple no longer attracts either become wholly sceptical and indifferent, or, as is often the case, transfer their allegiance to the new humanitarian doctrine which is fast assuming the character of a religion in the ardor it inspires and the strong spiritual union it cements. For the great body of the Jews, however, the central doctrine of Judaism remains unshaken, and doubtless, so long as Christianity exists, Judaism as a distinct creed will coëxist with it. The modern Jews, like their ancestors, believe that their mission is not yet ended, and they await with patience the rising of some new man of genius amongst them, who will combine the qualities of the popular leader with the attributes of the scholar, and will give body and form to the ideas elaborated by the Reformers. As a religious society they desire to remain distinct. But as citizens, they are eager to remove whatever distinctions still hamper their intercourse with their neighbors of other creeds. Never has the desire to return to Palestine and retrieve their lost nationality been more foreign to their sentiments than at the present day, though recent speculations have misled many to

[1] In an article on the religious aspects of the social question.

believe otherwise. They know they can no more return thither. They would not if they could. They love the land of their birth; they wish to join their labors with those of others in promoting the progress of the entire human race. They have ceased to regret the past, and desire nothing more earnestly than to live in the present and for the future.

THE END.

Religion in America
Series II

An Arno Press Collection

Adler, Felix. **Creed and Deed:** A Series of Discourses. New York, 1877.

Alexander, Archibald. **Evidences of the Authenticity, Inspiration, and Canonical Authority of the Holy Scriptures.** Philadelphia, 1836.

Allen, Joseph Henry. **Our Liberal Movement in Theology:** Chiefly as Shown in Recollections of the History of Unitarianism in New England. 3rd edition. Boston, 1892.

American Temperance Society. **Permanent Temperance Documents of the American Temperance Society.** Boston, 1835.

American Tract Society. **The American Tract Society Documents,** 1824-1925. New York, 1972.

Bacon, Leonard. **The Genesis of the New England Churches.** New York, 1874.

Bartlett, S[amuel] C. **Historical Sketches of the Missions of the American Board.** New York, 1972.

Beecher, Lyman. **Lyman Beecher and the Reform of Society:** Four Sermons, 1804-1828. New York, 1972.

[Bishop, Isabella Lucy Bird.] **The Aspects of Religion in the United States of America.** London, 1859.

Bowden, James. **The History of the Society of Friends in America.** London, 1850, 1854. Two volumes in one.

Briggs, Charles Augustus. **Inaugural Address and Defense,** 1891-1893. New York, 1972.

Colwell, Stephen. **The Position of Christianity in the United States,** in Its Relations with Our Political Institutions, and Specially with Reference to Religious Instruction in the Public Schools. Philadelphia, 1854.

Dalcho, Frederick. **An Historical Account of the Protestant Episcopal Church, in South-Carolina,** from the First Settlement of the Province, to the War of the Revolution. Charleston, 1820.

Elliott, Walter. **The Life of Father Hecker.** New York, 1891.

Gibbons, James Cardinal. **A Retrospect of Fifty Years.** Baltimore, 1916. Two volumes in one.

Hammond, L[ily] H[ardy]. **Race and the South:** Two Studies, 1914-1922. New York, 1972.

Hayden, A[mos] S. **Early History of the Disciples in the Western Reserve, Ohio;** With Biographical Sketches of the Principal Agents in their Religious Movement. Cincinnati, 1875.

Hinke, William J., editor. **Life and Letters of the Rev. John Philip Boehm:** Founder of the Reformed Church in Pennsylvania, 1683-1749. Philadelphia, 1916.

Hopkins, Samuel. **A Treatise on the Millennium.** Boston, 1793.

Kallen, Horace M. **Judaism at Bay:** Essays Toward the Adjustment of Judaism to Modernity. New York, 1932.

Kreider, Harry Julius. **Lutheranism in Colonial New York.** New York, 1942.

Loughborough, J. N. **The Great Second Advent Movement:** Its Rise and Progress. Washington, 1905.

M'Clure, David and Elijah Parish. **Memoirs of the Rev. Eleazar Wheelock, D.D.** Newburyport, 1811.

McKinney, Richard I. **Religion in Higher Education Among Negroes.** New Haven, 1945.

Mayhew, Jonathan. **Observations on the Charter and Conduct of the Society for the Propagation of the Gospel in Foreign Parts;** Designed to Shew Their Non-conformity to Each Other. Boston, 1763.

Mott, John R. **The Evangelization of the World in this Generation.** New York, 1900.

Payne, Bishop Daniel A. **Sermons and Addresses,** 1853-1891. New York, 1972.

Phillips, C[harles] H. **The History of the Colored Methodist Episcopal Church in America:** Comprising Its Organization, Subsequent Development, and Present Status. Jackson, Tenn., 1898.

Reverend Elhanan Winchester: Biography and Letters. New York, 1972.

Riggs, Stephen R. **Tah-Koo Wah-Kan; Or, the Gospel Among the Dakotas.** Boston, 1869.

Rogers, Elder John. **The Biography of Eld. Barton Warren Stone, Written by Himself:** With Additions and Reflections. Cincinnati, 1847.

Booth-Tucker, Frederick. **The Salvation Army in America:** Selected Reports, 1899-1903. New York, 1972.

Satolli, Francis Archbishop. **Loyalty to Church and State.** Baltimore, 1895.

Schaff, Philip. **Church and State in the United States** or the American Idea of Religious Liberty and its Practical Effects with Official Documents. New York and London, 1888. (Reprinted from *Papers of the American Historical Association,* Vol. II, No. 4.)

Smith, Horace Wemyss. **Life and Correspondence of the Rev. William Smith, D.D.** Philadelphia, 1879, 1880. Two volumes in one.

Spalding, M[artin] J. **Sketches of the Early Catholic Missions of Kentucky;** From Their Commencement in 1787 to the Jubilee of 1826-7. Louisville, 1844.

Steiner, Bernard C., editor. **Rev. Thomas Bray:** His Life and Selected Works Relating to Maryland. Baltimore, 1901. (Reprinted from *Maryland Historical Society Fund Publication,* No. 37.)

To Win the West: Missionary Viewpoints, 1814-1815. New York, 1972.

Wayland, Francis and H. L. Wayland. **A Memoir of the Life and Labors of Francis Wayland, D.D., LL.D.** New York, 1867. Two volumes in one.

Willard, Frances E. **Woman and Temperance:** Or, the Work and Workers of the Woman's Christian Temperance Union. Hartford, 1883.